Stuart Yarnold

BUILDING A PC

in
easy steps

Do it Yourself from Start to Finish

In easy steps is an imprint of Computer Step
Southfield Road · Southam
Warwickshire CV47 0FB · United Kingdom
www.ineasysteps.com

Second Edition

Notice of Liability
Every effort has been made to ensure that this book contains accurate and current information. However, Computer Step and the author shall not be liable for any loss or damage suffered by readers as a result of any information contained herein.

Trademarks
Microsoft® and Windows® are registered trademarks of Microsoft Corporation. All other trademarks are acknowledged as belonging to their respective companies.

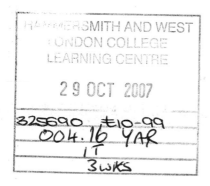
Printed and bound in the United Kingdom

ISBN-13 978-1-84078-326-1
ISBN-10 1-84078-326-5

Contents

1 Before You Start

This chapter will give you some useful information to help you buy the components you need and from the right sources, in order to build the perfect computer.

Introduction

So, you want to build yourself a computer. OK then, take a good look at the following picture:

Hot tip

Before you make a start on this project, consider the following:

Hardware technology is currently advancing at a much greater pace than software technology is. If you build a system using all the latest cutting-edge devices, such as 64-bit and dual-core CPUs, DDR2 RAM and PCI-Express video cards, you are going to have a system with a processing power that very few current software applications will be able to fully utilize. It will also be very expensive.

So, before you buy the parts, make sure that you really need the features, functions and power that they provide. Otherwise you'll be spending money to no good purpose.

These are all the components required to build a computer system. As you can see, there are quite a few of them, and while putting them all together may seem a somewhat daunting prospect, this stage is actually relatively straightforward.

Building a computer also involves two other stages – buying the parts and then having assembled them, setting up your system.

Regarding the former, there are many factors to consider and any mistakes at this stage can result in a computer system that, at best, is not what you really wanted it to be and, at worst, simply won't work.

For example, the central processing unit must be compatible with the motherboard and given the proliferation of motherboards, CPU socket types, etc, it is very easy to get this wrong.

To ensure you make the right decisions and do not end up with problems down the line, this book offers detailed buying guidelines regarding all the major parts in your system.

We then show you the correct way to install them. While this is not difficult, there are certain things you need to watch out for. A good example is the installation of the memory modules. You need to be very careful when doing this as it is very easy to destroy them by incorrect handling.

Liberal use of pictures helps to illustrate the assembly stage as clearly as possible. By the time you have finished, you should be looking at something like this:

Beware

Before you start, be aware that there are potential pitfalls with building a computer.
Horror of horrors, it might not work – then you will be faced with possibly a major troubleshooting exercise.

Hot tip

Computers are modular in construction. This helps to make the assembly stage relatively straightforward.

Finally, you need to set the system up. This will involve altering settings in the BIOS, partitioning and formatting the hard drive and installing the operating system and device drivers.

Many, if not most, problems are encountered at this stage, so this book gives full instructions on how to access and set up the BIOS, and get the hard drive operational.

Finally, you will find a chapter on troubleshooting common problems; this will be very useful should you find your new system does not work as expected.

Hot tip

Setting up the system and getting everything to work will, for most people, be the most difficult part of the job.

Store-Bought versus Self-Build

Before you decide to take the DIY route and start spending your hard-earned cash on all the various parts, give some thought to the pros and cons. Building a PC yourself can turn out to be an expensive mistake if things go wrong. Also, remember there are good reasons for buying from a store. These include:

Time

Self-build is going to take a lot longer than simply walking into your nearest store, buying a system off the shelf and then taking it home. To make it cost-effective you will have to spend time finding the cheapest suppliers of all the various parts, which will probably mean dealing with several different ones.

Effort

You have to actually build the PC, set it up and install the operating system.

Aggravation

If the completed system does not work then you have to troubleshoot it. This will take more time and, if it turns out you have damaged a component during assembly, it will need replacing at extra cost to you.

In addition, if you are unable to get the system working, you may end up taking it to a repair shop. All of this is going to involve more time and money. Buying from a store spares you all this potential aggravation.

System Warranty

A pre-built system comes with a warranty, a self-built system does not. If things go wrong, you're on your own. Buying from a store will give you peace of mind.

The advantages of self-build are:

Cost

If you buy OEM parts (see page 13), and from the right source, your PC should be cheaper than buying the ready-built equivalent. However, it must be said that the difference will probably not be as much as you might think and, if saving money is your primary motive, you may find it is simply not worth the bother.

Component Warranties

If you take the self-build route, you will at least have the warranties supplied with all the individual components. These are usually worth more than the PC manufacturers' warranties. Also service from component manufacturers is usually much swifter and more reliable.

Quality

It is a fact that most ready-built systems, particularly at the lower-end of the market, include parts of low quality. Typical examples are monitors and power supply units. Self-build allows you to choose good quality components that will give you a more reliable and longer lasting computer.

Design

Buy a PC from a store and you will, in all likelihood, be buying things you do not need or want. For example, it may come with a powerful processor, which will add considerably to its cost. However, if you only use the PC for applications that do not require much processing power, e.g. word-processing, email, etc, you will have wasted some of your money.

By building it yourself, you end up with a system that is tailored exactly to your requirements with no superfluous features or capabilities that will never be used.

Software

Most ready-built systems come with an operating system pre-installed. In addition, there will often be other software bundled with the system. However, this bundled software is often of dubious quality and usually also well past its sell-by date. Much of it is useless to the buyer and so is money wasted.

Many manufacturers these days supply PCs with the operating system in the form of a "recovery disk", rather than an original CD. This is fine as long as the operating system works. However, should you ever need to reinstall it, or do a new "clean" installation, you could well run into problems.

While, with the self-build route, you may have the additional expense of buying the operating system, it will at least be an original copy that can be used as many times as necessary.

Hot tip

Building your own computer allows you to "future-proof" it to a certain degree. For example, you can choose a motherboard that can take a more powerful CPU than the one you are intending to install. A year or so down the line, when the faster CPUs have dropped in price, you can then upgrade it.

11

Don't forget

There are few things as satisfying as tackling a difficult task and ending up with a successful result. Building your own computer definitely falls into this category.

What Do You Want it to Do?

Don't forget

Before you buy the parts, think about possible future uses for the PC.

This may save you money in the long-term by not having to make an early upgrade.

Having made the decision to build the PC yourself, you now need to make a list of all the parts required. This stage of building a computer is probably the most important, as any mistakes here will result in a PC that is not ideal (the whole point of the exercise) or that has to be subsequently modified at extra cost.

However, before you can do this you must establish exactly what you are going to use the PC for, i.e. the applications you intend to run. You then need to buy hardware (CPU, memory, etc.) that will be able to run these applications. The table below shows the approximate hardware requirements for some common applications.

Application	Example	CPU	RAM	Disk Space
Operating Systems	Windows XP Windows Vista	500 MHz 800 MHz	256 MB 512 MB	1.5 GB 9 GB
Office Suite	Microsoft Office 2007	500 MHz	256 MB	2 GB
Desktop Publishing	Adobe InDesign CS 3.0	500 MHz	256 MB	850 MB
Graphics Editor	Corel Paint Shop Pro 9	300 MHz	256 MB	500 MB
Games	Quake 4	2.0 GHz	512 MB	3.0 GB
Media Player	RealNetworks Real Player Plus	350 MHz	64 MB	52 MB
DVD Playback	Orion DirectDVD 6	1 GHz	128 MB	50 MB
CD/DVD Mastering	Roxio Easy Media Creator 9	500 MHz	128 MB	1 GB

Hot tip

With regard to Windows Vista, be aware that in order to run the new Aero (transparent windows) feature, a video system capable of supporting DirectX 9, Pixel Shader 2.0 and 128 MB of memory will be required.

Furthermore, while Vista can run with 512 MB of RAM, it will not perform at its full potential. To achieve this, you will need 1 GB of RAM.

With regard to CPUs, even the slowest model currently on the market will be capable of handling virtually any single application. However, you must remember that in practice you will be running two or more applications simultaneously.

So, for example, if you intend to play Quake 4 on a Windows Vista PC, you will need a CPU rated at a minimum of 2.8 GHz and at least 1 GB of memory. Also, there may well be other applications running in the background that you are not aware of; these will also be using the CPU and memory.

Regarding hard drive capacity, the only application that currently has an unusually high requirement is Windows Vista.

OEM versus Retail

Having drawn up your list of required components, it is time to go shopping. One of your first decisions is whether to buy retail or OEM products.

OEM stands for "Original Equipment Manufacturer" and is a term used to describe a company that manufactures hardware to be marketed under another company's brand name. Typically, OEM products are sold unboxed and with no documentation or bundled software. Also, warranties offered are usually limited. All this enables these products to be sold at a lower price.

The retail versions, on the other hand, will be packaged and supplied with user manuals, registration cards and full warranties. Very often, the buyer will also get bundled software. Most importantly, retail products are far more likely to be the genuine article – remember, there are many counterfeit products on the market.

Retail products will also include things that OEM versions don't. For example, a retail CPU will include a heat sink and fan; the OEM version will not. Retail hard drives will include the interface cable; OEM drives won't.

Another important factor is that of quality. All production lines, whatever the product, produce a number of sub-standard items that nevertheless work. This is particularly so with silicon chips, which are to be found in virtually all PC components. In literally every production run, some chips will be superior to others, these are the ones that will be packaged and sold at retail prices. Inferior chips go the OEM route.

Therefore, if you are looking to build a high quality system, you will definitely need to buy retail boxed components.

If budget is your primary concern, then buy OEM. You will save money, but it could be at the expense of quality. As with all things in life, you get what you pay for.

Something else to be wary of when buying OEM, is that many retailers, computer stores in particular, will try to sell you an OEM component at the full retail price. No one who is computer savvy will fall for this, but many people are caught out and end up paying the full price for an incomplete and sometimes inferior product.

Beware

If you buy OEM parts, be aware that in many cases, you will be buying extremely limited warranties. There is also a risk of getting fake or sub-standard components. Only take this route if you need to save money.

Don't forget

If you want parts guaranteed to be of good quality, spend the extra needed to get retail boxed products. It could save you money in the long run, not to mention unwanted aggravation.

Beware

If you do decide to buy any OEM products, make sure that you are not being conned into paying the full retail price. Be especially wary when buying OEM parts from a store.

Where to Buy Your Parts

Computer Stores

Buying from a store is probably your quickest and safest option. If a part is defective, you can simply take it back and exchange it for a new one. However, it does mean getting off your backside, and does not offer the convenience afforded by the mail order and Internet methods of shopping.

It is a known fact that sales staff in many of these stores, particularly the large chain-stores, can be somewhat limited in their knowledge of computers. Any advice or opinions offered by these people should be taken with a pinch of salt and checked out before you part with your cash.

There is also the risk of being conned into paying the full price for outdated items. While, to be fair, this can also happen with mail order and Internet companies, in practice, it is less likely as these companies exist by undercutting the big computer stores and will take every opportunity to do so.

You will pay the highest price for your components in computer stores, as they have high overheads to cover.

Mail Order

Mail order is very convenient and allows the buyer to compare prices without having to trudge from store to store. In addition, you do not have to keep fending off pushy sales staff.

You will usually find that a mail order catalog has a much wider range of products than you would find in any computer store.

Sales staff tend to be more knowledgeable about the products they are selling and will usually give you better advice than you would get in a store.

Prices will be lower than store prices and this is mail order's main advantage.

Disadvantages include time and distance. The company's headquarters could be several hundred miles away, so if there is a problem you cannot just nip down and get it sorted out immediately. Delivery is done by courier and it is quite common for delivered goods to arrive in a damaged condition. This means delays while the item is reshipped.

Hot tip

Before setting foot in a retail store, bone-up on the technical details of the product in which you are interested.

This will help you to understand what the sales staff are talking about. You will also come across as computer literate, making it less likely that they will try to put one over on you.

Hot tip

You need to be clued-up about the latest versions of any products in which you are interested. Otherwise, you may end up buying last year's model and possibly paying today's price for it.

Manufacturers' websites are the place to check for the latest products.

Another drawback is lack of information. Whereas in a computer store you can get a lot of facts from the box and associated promotional literature, not to mention actually seeing the product, the details in many catalogs can be on the sketchy side.

The Internet

The Internet has become a real boon to those who build and upgrade PCs. Not only can you buy your parts at the lowest price online, but you can also get a tremendous amount of information to help you make informed buying decisions.

There are sites devoted to all the major parts of a computer system. These offer information such as technical details, troubleshooting, installation and buying guides, etc.
If you are looking for detailed specifications on a particular product, visit the manufacturer's website; all the major manufacturers are now online.

Also online are the major computer and computer parts retailers. Their online prices are lower than in their retail outlets.

Price comparison sites, such as www.pricewatch.com in the USA and www.kelkoo.com in Europe, are very useful.

Simply key in the relevant details and you will be presented with a list of sites selling the product, together with the price. This can save a lot of time when looking for the best deal.

Another advantage is that online catalogs are usually much more detailed in terms of specifications and features than mail order catalogs.

In all other respects though, buying on the Internet is the same as buying mail order. It all relies on courier and postal delivery, and is subject to the same limitations and restrictions.

Don't forget

Mail order catalogs and the Internet give you access to a much wider range of products than you are likely to find in any retail outlet. In addition, you will have no sales staff to keep at arms length, so you can browse at your leisure.

Beware

Many websites offer products at seemingly bargain prices that do not actually exist. This is a common ruse to get you interested in the site. Sites selling bargain holidays and flights are typical offenders in this respect, and some computer-related sites use the same trick.

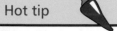

Hot tip

Many motherboards come with integrated sound and video systems. If you don't need high quality sound and video, these will be perfectly adequate.

Don't forget

A toolkit is not necessary to build a PC.

Parts You Will Need

The following is a list of the hardware components you will need to build a basic computer system:

- Monitor
- System case
- Power supply unit (PSU)
- Motherboard
- Central processing unit (CPU)
- Memory (RAM)
- Hard drive
- Video card (see top margin note)
- Sound card (see top margin note)
- Floppy drive
- CD or DVD drive
- Keyboard
- Mouse
- Speakers

Tools You Will Need

Very little is required in the way of tooling. The following is all you are likely to need:

Screwdrivers
One medium size cross-head screwdriver for screwing the motherboard into place and securing the drive units and expansion cards.

Needle-Nose Pliers
This will come in handy for relocating hard drive jumpers. If you do not have one though, a pair of tweezers will be adequate.

Cutter
For cutting cable ties to length. You will need these to bundle up the internal cables in a neat fashion, so they do not interfere with airflow in the case. You will also need a supply of cable ties. These are available from any computer store.

Electrostatic Wrist Strap
This item is not essential, but is highly recommended. The static electricity in your body is a killer for the PC's circuit boards; this applies particularly to the memory modules.

2 Central Processing Units

This chapter will clear up some of the misconceptions regarding these devices, show you which section of the market you should be looking at and explain associated terminology and technology.

CPU Manufacturers

Along with the motherboard, the processor is one of the most important parts in a PC and, more than any other, influences the speed at which it runs.

There are quite a few CPU manufacturers, the more well known being AMD, Intel, IBM, Compaq, SIS and Via. IBM and Compaq processors are aimed more at the business end of the market, while Via and SIS are better known for their chipsets, which are found on many mainstream motherboards.

Therefore, as far as the home-PC market and the self-builder are concerned, the choice comes down to Intel or AMD. Both companies make models for high-end, mid-range and low-end machines.

Intel

For a long time Intel dominated the processor market, which could explain why its prices are generally higher than comparable offerings from AMD.

Its high-end CPUs are the Xeon and the Itanium, which are aimed at the Server market. These are seriously high-performance processors and are priced accordingly. For the self-builder they do not really come into the equation.

Of more interest is the Pentium. This comes in a range of speeds up to a current maximum of 3.8 GHz. The Pentium family includes the traditional single-core processor and the more recent dual-core models that are now becoming extremely popular. Both types are available in 64-bit versions as well.

Courtesy of Intel Corporation

For gamers demanding extreme performance levels, there is the Pentium D Extreme 955 CPU.

Finally, there is the Celeron, which is essentially a budget version of the Pentium and accordingly offers lower performance levels. Note that there is also a 64-bit version of this CPU.

Beware

There is a lot of marketing hype regarding the clock speed of CPUs. However, this is only one indicator of a CPU's quality. You should also consider things like the size of the Level-2 cache, Front Side Bus (FSB) speed, the chip's micron size, and technology such as Hyper-Threading, Quantispeed architecture and Thermal Monitoring.

As ever though, the best indicator of all is the price.

AMD

With the introduction of their Athlon family of processors in 1999, Advanced Micro Devices (AMD), began a serious challenge to Intel's dominance of the market.

Their success has been due in no small part to the fact that AMD processors are mostly cheaper than their Intel equivalents, while still delivering the same level of performance – many would say AMD processors perform better.

AMD's top of the range model is currently the Opteron and, as with Intel's Xeon and Itanium, this is aimed at the business end of the market.

Next is the Athlon; this is the chip that will be of interest to the self-builder. As with Intel's Pentium, there are single-core, dual-core and 64-bit versions of this CPU.

To keep gamers happy AMD supply the high-performance Athlon 64 FX 55.

AMD's budget CPU is the Sempron and this processor competes with Intel's Celeron.

In general, the performance levels of Athlon CPUs are broadly similar to Intel's Pentium.

The table below gives a comparison.

Intel		AMD
Celeron	equivalent	Sempron
Pentium	equivalent	Athlon
Xeon/Itanium	equivalent	Opteron

Given that, performance wise, there is little to choose between AMD and Intel processors, the determining factor for most people is the price.

Don't forget

There are two distinct markets for CPUs; the desktop market and the business market.

CPUs aimed at the desktop market are Intel's Celeron and Pentium, while AMD's offerings are the Sempron and the Athlon.

For the business market, Intel offers the Xeon and Itanium, and AMD have the Opteron.

Don't forget

The only real difference between CPUs from Intel and AMD is the price. In all other respects they are much the same.

Performance Ratings

Performance ratings are intended to enable the buyer to quickly evaluate the performance level of a CPU.

AMD

To understand AMD's method, you have to first realize that their CPUs run at a lower clock speed than Intel's. However, the performance is the same as the equivalent Intel CPUs (this is because AMD CPUs have a higher instruction per cycle rating, which means that they do more per clock cycle than Intel's).

Therefore, if they advertise their CPUs at the true clock speed, they would appear to be considerably slower than Intel's and buyers would thus go for the Intel CPU.

To prevent this, mainstream AMD CPUs are advertised with a performance rating that tells the buyer which Intel CPU is the equivalent in terms of performance. For example, an AMD Athlon 64 3200 (3200 is the rating) has a true clock speed of 2.0 GHz. However, it gives the same level of performance as an Intel Pentium 4 641 with a clock speed of 3.2 GHz.

Intel

Until recently, Intel simply advertised their CPUs at the clock speed. However, as clock speed is only one indicator of a CPUs performance – there are several others (see pages 23-24), they have now introduced a performance rating of their own.

This removes references to individual specifications and replaces them with a three-digit number (735 in the example below).

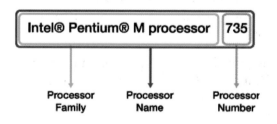

This number relates to Cache, Architecture, Clock Speed and Front Side Bus (FSB).

However, to derive anything from it you need to go to the Intel website (www.intel.com/products/processor_number/info.htm) and look it up.

As a quick means of evaluation it actually tells you nothing and so CPU suppliers are still advertising the clock speed, cache size and FSB speed as they were before the rating was introduced.

see pages 23-24

Don't forget

When comparing CPUs from Intel and AMD, ignore the clock speed figure for AMD's CPUs. Instead, focus on the performance rating figure, e.g. 2800, 3200, etc.

What CPU To Buy?

All desktop PCs can be placed in one of four categories: low-end, mid-range, high-end, and gaming machines. The CPU you buy will, to a large degree, be dictated by which of these categories your PC is intended to be in.

High-End Systems
This type of system is typically used in one of two ways:

Multi-Tasking
Multi-tasking is where several applications are run simultaneously. Individually, they may not be CPU intensive but collectively they will be. There are two options:

- A dual-core processor. This is the best choice. Here, the CPU has two separate processors, each of which handles half the workload, thus giving the system a major boost

- A Hyper-Thread CPU. By means of some clever circuitry, these CPUs appear to the system as two separate CPUs, and to a certain degree, act as two. While not as good as a dual-core CPU, they are the next best thing

Running a Single CPU Intensive Application
Systems running a single CPU intensive application do not need a dual-core CPU. Here, the choice will be a high-end single-core CPU running at 3.0 GHz or higher.

Mid-Range Systems
These PCs tend to be used for a range of applications, some need a reasonably powerful CPU and others don't. For example, PC games that aren't too CPU intensive (not all of them are), office applications, email and the Internet.

These will all run very nicely with a mid-range CPU rated from 2.5 to 3.0 GHz. Intel's Pentium 4, AMD's Athlon 64, and faster versions of the Sempron and Celeron will all be suitable.

Low-End Systems
Basic applications such as word-processing, playing FreeCell, email and web browsing require very little from the CPU.

The choice here will be low-end Celerons from Intel and Semprons from AMD. These are the cheapest CPUs on the market and will be quite adequate for this type of use.

Hot tip

An important factor to remember when buying a CPU is your possible requirements in the future. While you may not need a powerful one now, you may subsequently develop an interest that does require more processing power. For this reason, it makes sense to buy one with "a bit in hand".

...cont'd

Hot tip

As a rule of thumb, AMD's CPUs provide better gaming performance, while Intel's are faster at general PC applications.

High-Performance Gaming Machines

For the hardcore gamer, there can be no compromises – the PC is set up with one purpose in mind – playing 3D games with "all guns blazing".

To get the best out of these games in terms of frame rate (speed), and graphic and sound options, a seriously powerful CPU will be required.

AMD and Intel both supply one designed specifically for gaming machines.

Currently, Intel's offering is the Pentium D Extreme 955. This is a dual-core CPU with each core running at 3.4 GHz and having a 2 MB L2 cache. The presence of dual-core technology makes it also suitable for heavy multi-tasking.

AMD's is the Athlon 64 FX 55. This is also a dual-core CPU with each core having a clock speed of 2.6 GHz and 1 MB of L2 cache.

Both of these CPUs are entering the market at the time of writing, and the early reviews suggest that the Pentium D Extreme 955 has the edge on performance.

Hot tip

Note that the two CPUs mentioned opposite are currently the best choice for hardcore gamers. By the time you are reading this, however, the situation may have changed.

Specifications

Now that you know what type of CPU is required in relation to your intended use of the PC, the next task is to choose one that will do the job. This means looking at the specifications. The following are the ones that should be considered:

Clock Speed

This is the speed at which a CPU runs and is measured as a frequency, e.g. 2.0 GHz or 2000 million cycles per second. As every action (instruction) carried out by the CPU requires one or more cycles, it follows that the higher the clock speed, the more actions it will be able to carry out in any given second.

You need to be aware though, that there is a lot more to a CPU's performance than just clock speed. For example, you can buy a 3.0 GHz version of both the Celeron and the Pentium 4: the Celeron, however, costs considerably less and you can be quite sure that it is not going to perform nearly as well despite having the same clock speed. The following specifications show why.

Front Side Bus (FSB)

A very important CPU specification is the speed at which it communicates with the rest of the PC; this is commonly known as the Front Side Bus speed, or just FSB.

Going back to our Pentium 4/Celeron example above, the 3.0 GHz Pentium 4 has an FSB of 800 MHz, while the 3.0 GHz Celeron has one of 533 MHz. So although they both have the same processing power, the Pentium 4 can transfer data to the system much more quickly as it has a faster FSB.

For the CPU's FSB to be effective, however, it must be supported by the motherboard. If the motherboard can't run at that speed, i.e. its own FSB is lower, data transfer between the CPU and the system will be at the lower speed, i.e. the motherboard's. Therefore, the system will not be able to fully utilize the CPU's processing power.

So before buying your CPU, check that its FSB is supported by the motherboard you intend to buy (or vice versa). To make life a bit easier for users, virtually all motherboards support several FSB speeds (usually three). When the CPU is installed, the motherboard will automatically detect its speed and configure itself to run at the same speed.

Don't forget

CPUs, memory, and motherboards are all built to communicate with the rest of the system at a specific speed. This is known as the Front Side Bus (FSB).

It's important to realize that these three components must all be able to run at the same speed in order to get the maximum performance from them.

If one runs at a lower speed, effectively, it becomes a performance bottleneck.

Cache Memory

Cache memory is an area of high-speed memory built-in to the CPU, which is used to store frequently accessed data. Since this data doesn't have to be retrieved from the much slower RAM, overall performance is improved considerably. Going back to the Pentium 4/Celeron comparison once again, the Pentium 4 typically, has two to four times as much cache memory as does the Celeron.

Note that CPUs commonly use two types of cache – level 1 (L1) and level 2 (L2). L2 is slightly slower than L1 but is larger, and is the one usually specified by vendors.

Other factors to consider, include:

Compatibility – the CPU connects to the PC via a socket on the motherboard. However, different processors use different types of socket, so you must establish that your chosen CPU is physically compatible with the socket on your intended motherboard. This is simple enough – the socket it uses will be specified in the CPU specifications, and the motherboard specifications will specify the CPU socket supplied.

Cooling – CPUs generate a lot of heat and so must be adequately cooled by a suitable heatsink/fan assembly to prevent them from burning out. If you buy a retail CPU, this won't be a problem – an approved unit will be included. However, if you buy an OEM CPU, you will have to buy one separately. The important thing here is to make sure that the heatsink/fan assembly you buy is recommended for use with the CPU. If it is not, you could well have heat related problems down the line.

Power – this will be a consideration only if you are buying one of the latest high-end CPUs. These devices draw a lot of power, so you must make sure that the power supply unit (PSU) is up to the job (see page 69).

Technology – Intel and AMD both employ various technologies, such as Hyper-Transport and Hyper-Threading on certain of their processors. These make a considerable difference to both the performance and the price of the CPUs in question. We'll look at these technologies next.

Technologies

Hyper-Transport

Hyper-Transport technology is unique to AMD CPUs, and is basically a high-speed, low-power communication channel (bus) that allows the CPU to communicate with the system at a faster speed and thus with greater data throughput.

CPUs that employ it have two data channels – first to communicate with memory and, second (the Hyper-Transport bus) to communicate with the motherboard chipset. Thus, these CPUs can communicate with both the memory and the chipset simultaneously – CPUs without Hyper-Transport cannot do this as they have only one communication channel.

Another advantage of the Hyper-Transport bus is that it provides a route for the transmission of data and a separate route for its reception. In the traditional architecture used by other processors, a single route is used both for the transmission and for the reception of data.

Users who will be interested in Hyper-Transport CPUs are those who run applications that require seriously high data transfer speeds, such as video-editing, CAD, 3D animation, etc.

Hyper-Threading

Not to be confused with AMD's Hyper-Transport, Hyper-Threading is an Intel technology that offers improved multi-tasking performance by creating a virtual CPU that appears to the operating system as a second CPU. This allows it to handle two processes simultaneously.

Intel claims up to a 30 per cent speed improvement in comparison to an otherwise identical Pentium 4. The performance gain achieved is very application dependent, however, and some programs actually slow down slightly when used with a Hyper-Thread CPU.

Is it worth having? If you do serious multi-tasking, the answer is yes. Otherwise, no.

Note that for Hyper-Threading to function properly, it must be supported not only by the motherboard, but also by the application being run.

In essence, it is a poor man's dual-core CPU – cheaper but not as effective.

...cont'd

Hot tip

To avoid the need for an early upgrade, it makes sense to fit your new PC with a 64-bit, dual-core CPU.

Don't forget

A 64-bit CPU will run 32-bit applications. So you can install one, run your existing applications, and then replace them with 64-bit versions as and when they become available.

Beware

Don't confuse dual-core with dual-processor. A dual-processor system has two separate CPUs, each of which has its own hardware. Thus, it provides much better performance than a dual-core CPU, which has to share associated hardware, such as the memory controller and front side bus.

64-Bit Architecture

This is the latest technology to hit the desktop market; 64-bit CPUs are able to process data much more quickly than traditional 32-bit CPUs.

A 64-bit CPU has the power to dramatically improve the performance of CPU-intensive applications, such as audio and video encoding, complex engineering programs like CAD, and games. There are issues though:

- 64-bit CPUs are currently quite expensive (although prices are dropping fast)

- To gain the full advantages offered, software (including the operating system and hardware drivers) needs to be 64-bit compatible. So anyone buying a 64-bit CPU will also need to buy a complete new set of 64-bit software. It is also a fact that, currently, there are few 64-bit capable applications on the market

Do you need it? For the majority of users, at the moment the answer has to be no. A 64-bit system offers a level of performance that is basically an overkill – most current applications are simply not capable of fully utilizing it. That said, it won't be long before future applications, particularly games, will need a 64-bit system for optimum performance and so we recommend that you future-proof your system by fitting a 64-bit CPU in your new PC. In the meantime, it can still run your current 32-bit applications.

Dual-Core

A recent innovation in the desktop market, dual-core CPUs employ two processor cores on the same chip. Each core functions and processes data independently and the two are coordinated by the operating system. The main advantage this offers is much improved multi-tasking and, to a lesser extent, increased performance for multi-thread applications.

Dual-core CPUs are not cheap and offer performance levels that, currently, most users do not need. However, as with 64-bit technology, it won't be long before mainstream applications appear that do need it, so to avoid the need for an early upgrade, we would advise you to fit your new PC with a dual-core CPU now.

Installing a CPU

The steps in this section show an AMD Athlon CPU being installed. The procedure is exactly the same for an Intel CPU. Whichever you use, just remember that CPUs are fragile devices and successful installation will require a delicate touch.

1   Lift the socket-locking lever to the 90-degree position

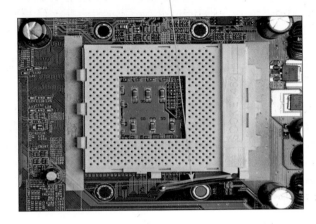

27

Hot tip

The locking lever is part of the Zero Insertion Force (ZIF) mechanism, which opens the socket's pin holes to accept the CPU.

2   Align the two triangular corners of the CPU with the corresponding corners of the socket

Hot tip

AMD processors have two diagonal corners and a gold triangle stamped on both sides of one corner. This is to ensure the CPU cannot be installed the wrong way round.

    Intel processors have a gold triangle stamped on the front of the CPU and two pins removed on the business end.

...cont'd

Beware

Never try to force a CPU into its socket. If you do, you will bend, and possibly break, the pins. Wiggle it about slightly to line the pins up with the socket holes and it will then drop easily into place.

Beware

Before closing the locking lever, have a good look at all four sides of the CPU to make sure they are flush with the socket.

 Drop the CPU into the socket

 Close the locking lever

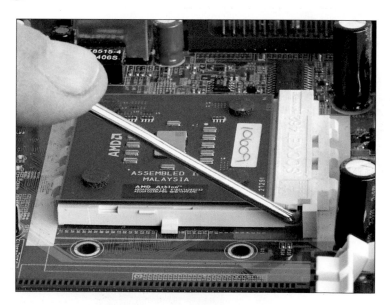

The next stage is to fit the heatsink/fan assembly. Without it, the CPU will rapidly overheat and eventually burn out.

Fitting a Heatsink and Fan

The first thing to mention here is the importance of using a thermal compound between the CPU and the heatsink. This greatly aids the transfer of heat away from the CPU (see top margin note). Without it, the CPU may well overheat.

Intel Heatsinks

Intel heatsinks are very easy to fit as they simply clip on to a retention frame that surrounds the CPU's socket.

Hot tip

New heatsinks are supplied with a thermal pad in situ, as shown below. Be careful to keep your fingers off it as dead skin and oil reduces its effectiveness.

Mounted on the heatsink itself is a clip assembly, which engages with the retention frame.

1 Align the heatsink with the retention frame and simply press down; it should snap into place

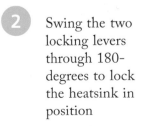

2 Swing the two locking levers through 180-degrees to lock the heatsink in position

Don't forget

Don't forget to close the assembly locking levers; this is something that is easily overlooked. Finally, connect the CPU fan to the motherboard.

AMD Heatsinks

Heatsink/fan assemblies for AMD CPUs are more awkward to fit as considerable force can be required to engage the locking clips.

 1 Check that there is a thermal strip or paste on the bottom of the heatsink

2 Align the recess at the bottom of the heatsink with the corresponding lip on the socket

3 Engage the locking clip on one side of the heatsink with the matching lug on the socket

4 Engage the clip on the other side of the heatsink (you may need a flat-head screwdriver to force it into place)

3 Memory

Memory comes in a range of types, versions and speeds, and picking the right one can be confusing for the uninitiated. Here, you'll learn all you need to know about memory so that you make the correct choice. We'll also show you how to handle and install memory modules.

Overview

As with the CPU, the system memory (RAM) is a component that has a major impact on the performance of a computer system. You can install the fastest processor in the world, but without an adequate amount of memory, all that processing power will do you no good at all.

The memory market can be extremely confusing for the uninitiated as there are many different types, e.g. SDRAM, DDR SDRAM, Registered, Unbuffered, ECC, Rambus, etc.

To further muddy the waters, they come in a range of speeds and technologies. SDRAM memory modules, for example, operate at various speeds, e.g. 100, 133, 166, 200 MHz. However, a different type of SDRAM, DDR (double data rate) SDRAM, effectively doubles these speeds – a DDR module rated at a speed of 133 MHz will actually operate at 266 MHz.

Then there is the question of RAM form factors. The form factor of any memory module describes its size and pin configuration. Typical examples are SIMMs, DIMMs and RIMMs. Buy the wrong one and it will not physically fit in the motherboard.

When buying memory, you also have to consider the CPU and motherboard that will be used in conjunction with the memory. For the module to function at its best, its speed must match that of both these components.

If you intend to install a large amount of memory, you should be aware that there are limits, which are set by the motherboard. If you install more than the board can use, you will be wasting some of your money.

However, while all this may sound daunting, choosing the right memory for your PC is actually not too difficult, as we'll see.

Types of Memory

Double Data Rate SDRAM

The memory technology currently in favor is Double Data Rate Synchronous Dynamic RAM, otherwise known as DDR SDRAM. The majority of desktop PCs are now using this type of memory as it's cheap and fast. Unless you are looking for extreme levels of performance, this is probably what you will use.

In comparison to its predecessor (SDR SDRAM), DDR SDRAM transfers data much more quickly due to a technical modification, whereby data is transferred on both the up and down sides of a clock cycle. The table below lists the various versions that are available:

Version	Clock Speed (MHz)	FSB Speed (MHz)	Data Transfer Rate (GB/s)
PC2100	133	266	2.1
PC2400	150	300	2.4
PC2700	166	333	2.7
PC3000	183	366	3.0
PC3200	200	400	3.2
PC3500	216	433	3.5
PC3700	233	466	3.7
PC4000	250	500	4.0
PC4300	266	533	4.3

From this we can see that because both the up and down sides of a clock cycle are used, the FSB speed of the modules is twice that of the rated clock speed.

The transfer rate (also known as bandwidth) shows the amount of data transferred in one second.

DDR SDRAM is supplied in 184-pin DIMM modules as shown below.

For gamers and power users who want the ultimate in speed and reliability, DDR SDRAM is also available in high-performance modules. These are designed and built to very tight tolerances, undergo stringent testing, and are ideal for over-clocking (squeezing the last drop of performance by altering settings in the system's BIOS) – see margin note.

Hot tip

Overclocking is a technique used to make certain components (typically the CPU, memory and the video card) operate at speeds faster than intended by the manufacturer. This is done by the use of multipliers in the BIOS.

This is possible because manufacturers build in some spare capacity in their products so they don't run at "full stretch". Overclocking makes use of this spare capacity.

...cont'd

Typical high-performance modules are the XMS series from Corsair and the Hyper-X series from Kingston.

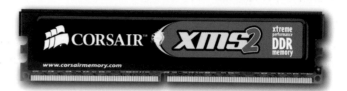

Double Data Rate 2 SDRAM

DDR2 SDRAM is an enhanced version of DDR SDRAM, and uses a modified signalling method to enable even higher speeds. These modules have a 240-pin edge connector, so they are incompatible with mainstream motherboards, which are designed to accept 184-pin DDR SDRAM modules. DDR2 SDRAM is currently available in the following versions:

Version	Clock Speed (MHz)	FSB Speed (MHz)	Data Transfer Rate (GB/s)
PC2-3200	200	400	3.2
PC2-4300	266	533	4.3
PC2-5400	333	667	5.4
PC2-6400	400	800	6.4
PC2-7200	450	900	7.2
PC2-8000	500	1000	8.0
PC2-8500	533	1066	8.5

As you can see from the table, DDR2 carries on where DDR left off. However, anyone who is considering using it should be aware of the following:

First, it has to be supported by the CPU and most of the CPUs that do are from Intel. The only AMD CPUs that support DDR2 are those that use AMD's new AM socket. So if you want your system to have a AMD CPU and DDR2 memory, you will be restricted to a few high-end (and expensive) CPUs.

Second, DDR2 is not supported by mainstream motherboards, which are designed for DDR. You will need a motherboard designed to accept DDR2 modules.

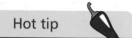

Hot tip

High-performance modules for gamers are also available in DDR2 SDRAM.

Hot tip

With DDR3 memory expected to be available in 2007, you may be better off fitting inexpensive DDR memory for now. This will be much cheaper to upgrade than DDR2 memory.

Error-Checking Memory

When investigating the memory market, you will also come across other, apparently different types of memory, such as Parity, ECC, etc. We'll take a brief look at these.

- Parity – parity modules have an extra (parity) chip for error detection. This checks that data is correctly read or written by the memory module by adding additional bits and using a special algorithm. However, it will not correct an error

- ECC – ECC modules are very similar to parity modules. However, unlike parity modules, the ECC module will, in most cases, correct any errors it finds, depending on the type of error

- Buffered – buffered modules contain a buffer chip to help the module cope with the large electrical load required for large amounts of memory. The buffer electrically isolates the memory from the controller to minimize the load on the chipset

- Registered – very similar to buffered memory, these modules contain registers that hold the data for one clock cycle before it is moved on to the motherboard

All of the above modules are based on SDRAM technology and are available in DDR and DDR2 versions. The difference between them and standard SDRAM memory is the fact that they incorporate some type of error-checking technique that increases their reliability (and hence that of the PC) considerably.

For this reason they are found predominantly in Servers and mission-critical systems.

The typical home PC has no need for these types of memory.

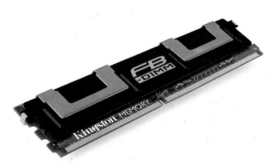

Drawbacks are that they are considerably more expensive and are also slower in operation (due to the error-checking procedure).

Beware

Error-checking memory is not compatible with mainstream motherboards. Boards that are tend to be very expensive.

Don't forget

The types of memory described on this page are not intended for use in a typical home PC. The only users who might have a need for them are those who do mission-critical work on their PC.

Buying Memory

When the time comes to make this decision, you should have already decided what type of system you want, i.e. low-, mid-, high-end or gaming, and chosen your motherboard and CPU accordingly. This is important, as to get the best out of your memory it must be compatible with these devices.

You need to consider the following:

Type of Memory

This is the first thing to decide and is a straightforward decision: DDR SDRAM or DDR2 SDRAM.

DDR SDRAM is cheap, fast and compatible with mainstream motherboards. For low- to mid-level systems, it is the obvious choice. If you are building a gaming or high-performance machine, go for the souped-up modules, such as Corsair's XMS and Kingston's Hyper-X.

If you want to be at the cutting-edge or need extreme performance then DDR2 SDRAM will be the choice. This will also ensure that your system is future-proofed as far as possible in relation to memory. Bear in mind that DDR3 is just round the corner, so if you want to stay at the sharp-end, you may be shelling out again rather sooner than you would like.

Whichever type you go for, if you need the highest possible level of reliability, you will need to buy error-checking modules as discussed on page 35.

Don't forget

For typical computer uses, you need look no further than DDR SDRAM. Performance enthusiasts will consider high-performance modules such as Kingston's Hyper-X.
Cutting-edge enthusiasts will be interested in DDR2 SDRAM.

Don't forget

DDR2 memory requires a compatible CPU (and these are the more recent and thus expensive models). You will also need to buy a motherboard that supplies 240-pin memory sockets.

FSB

For the best possible system performance, the memory's FSB must be the same as the CPU's, otherwise it becomes a performance bottleneck. The slower it is in relation to the CPU, the slower the system will be. However, modern CPUs have high FSBs, typically 800 MHz and higher, and the fastest mainstream DDR memory, PC4300, has an FSB of only 533 MHz. So what are your options? There are three:

1) Buy PC2-6400, and above, DDR2 modules. These do have CPU comparable FSBs (but are extremely expensive)

2) Use dual-channel memory. This requires a dual-channel enabled motherboard and a matched pair of identical memory modules. Theoretically, this doubles the memory's data transfer rate bringing it into line with the CPU. In practice, however, this doesn't happen and realistically, you can expect to achieve a memory speed increase of about 10-15 per cent

3) Settle for a trade-off in terms of cost versus performance

The memory's FSB also needs to be supported by the motherboard. The easiest way to ensure you get this right is to look at the motherboard's specifications, which you will find at the relevant manufacturer's website. An example is shown below.

Beware

If you install a memory module rated at a speed higher than the motherboard and CPU are designed to handle, the memory will still work but only at the motherboard's maximum FSB. You won't be getting the best out of it.

If you install a module rated at a speed lower than the motherboard or CPU FSB, this will create a bottleneck in the system as the memory will not be able to keep up. The result will be degraded system performance.

Boxed Intel® Desktop Board D915GUX	
Form Factor	Micro ATX (9.6" x 9.6")
Processor	• Support for the Intel® Pentium® 4 processor with Hyper-Threading in the LGA775 socket with an 800 MHz system bus • Supports boxed Intel desktop processors with packaging designated by 04B or 04A Platform Compatibility Guide.
Memory	• Four 240-pin DIMM connectors supporting up to four double-sided DIMMs • DDR2 533/400 SDRAM memory • Designed to support up to 4 GB^2 of system memory
Chipset	Intel® 915G Express Chipset
Security	• Infineon® Trusted Platform Module (optional) • Wave Systems® • EMBASSY® Trust Suite (optional) • Document Manager • Private Information Manager • SmartSignature®
Audio	Intel® High Definition Audio with flexible 6-channel audio and jack sensing
Video	• Intel® Graphics Media Accelerator 900 • PCI Express® x16 connector (with integrated retention mechanism) provides enhanced bandwidth for next-generation graphics card technology and future headroom
I/O Control	Integrated super I/O LPC bus controller

Peripheral Interfaces	• Up to eight USB 2.0 ports
	  • Four ports routed to the back panel
	  • Four ports routed to two USB headers
	• Four Serial ATA (SATA) channels, via the ICH6, one device per channel
	• One IDE interface with ATA-66/100 supporting up to two devices
	• One diskette drive interface
	• One parallel port
	• One serial port

Expansion Capabilities	• Two PCI connectors • One PCI Express® x1 connector
Network Interface	Intel® PRO 10/100 LAN or Gigabit Ethernet LAN (optional)

Don't forget

To work in dual-channel mode, the modules must be identical (many memory manufacturers sell dual-channel kits for this purpose). Dual-channel must also be supported by both the motherboard and CPU.

The specifications show you the type, speed, and amount of memory supported by the board.

...cont'd

Another method is to use the configurator tools provided by the memory manufacturers on their websites.

Latency

A key performance indicator, especially for high-end memory modules, is the speed at which the module can locate data. This is not to be confused with the data transfer speed, which is usually measured in GB/s, but the amount of time, in clock cycles, it takes a module to begin transferring the requested data.

When a PC's memory receives a request for data, it first has to determine which module contains the desired data. Then it has to switch to that module, which in turn has to determine which of the chips on its board contains the data, and then which bank of memory it is in. Finally, it has to call the memory forward before it can be put on the bus for transmission to the CPU. The time taken to do all this is known as latency.

Latency is measured in clock cycles and there are many factors involved such as tRAS, tRP, tRCD and command rate. However the most common, and most important, factor is known as CAS (Column Access Strobe).

In DDR SDRAM, CAS latency (sometimes called CL) will be 1.5, 2 or 2.5 clock cycles. In DDR2, it will be 3, 4 or 5. It specifies how many clock cycles the module will use to access the data in its chips. Fairly obviously, the lower the CAS latency, the better.

For example, a DDR memory module with a CAS latency of 1.5 will be approximately 5-10 per cent faster overall than one with a CAS of 2.5. Remember however, that this is relative: DDR2 has higher CAS latencies than DDR, but compensates by having faster clock cycles.

Memory Capacity

The amount of memory that you need in your system is determined by the applications that you intend to run. Don't forget that this also includes the operating system.

The table on the next page provides an approximate guide to the amount of memory required by typical applications.

Operating System	Low-Usage	Mid-Usage	High-Usage
Windows Vista	512 MB	1 GB	2 GB
Windows XP	256 MB	512 MB	1 GB
Windows Me	128 MB	256 MB	512 MB
Windows 98	64 MB	128 MB	256 MB
Windows 95	32 MB	64 MB	128 MB
Mac OS X	256 MB	512 MB	1 GB
Linux	256 MB	512 MB	1 GB

Low-usage is defined as resource light applications, such as word-processing, web browsing, email, 2D games, data-entry, etc. If you tend to run several of these applications simultaneously, you should install the amount specified in the mid-usage column.

Mid-usage is running programs such as photo-editing, web applications, multimedia, sound-editing, printing, scanning, etc. If you run several of these at the same time, install the amount specified in the high-usage column.

High-usage is defined as 3D gaming (particularly online gaming), real-time video-editing, computer aided design (CAD), animation, 3D modeling, high-end desktop publishing, etc.

Memory Manufacturers

Unlike the CPU, where the choice is essentially between Intel and AMD, both of whose products are high quality, there is any number of memory manufacturers.

As the memory plays a crucial role in the performance and reliability of a computer system, you must buy the best you can afford – this is not a component on which to economize.

Three manufacturers spring to mind here – Crucial, Corsair, and Kingston Technologies. Buy your memory from any of these companies and you won't go wrong.

Avoid cheap unbranded memory as you would the plague. Poor quality modules cause system crashes and lock-ups, not to mention loss of data.

Hot tip

Another consideration is your future memory requirements. Each succeeding version of Windows, and virtually all major software titles, require more memory than preceding versions did. For this reason, it makes sense to add a bit more to your system than you currently need.

Don't forget

For guaranteed quality, buy branded memory from well known manufacturers such as Kingston and Crucial.

Handling Memory Modules

Before you do anything, read the following paragraph:

The electrostatic electricity present in your body is absolutely lethal to memory chips. If you don't ground yourself to discharge it, just one touch can destroy the module.

So, if you have an electrostatic wriststrap now is the time to use it. Alternatively, touch the bare metal of the system case chassis. We also recommend that you avoid standing on a carpet – this is the best way to build up a static charge.

When you do pick up the chip, hold it by the edges as far as possible, as shown below:

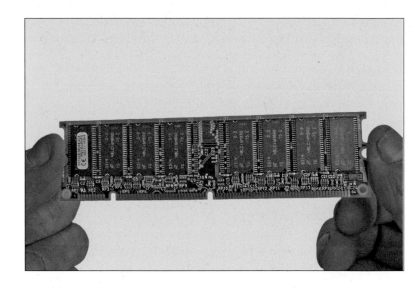

Another way to safeguard against electrostatic electricity is to buy a module that comes with a heat-spreader, as shown in the example below. This ensures that you cannot touch the circuitry inside.

Beware

Memory modules are the component most likely to be damaged by incorrect handling. Just one careless touch is all it takes, so be warned.

Don't forget

Memory modules are also available with a heat-spreader. While these are intended primarily as a means of dissipating heat, they also provide the added benefit of protection.

Installing Memory

1 The first thing to do is open the plastic retaining clips on each side of the slot/s you are going to use

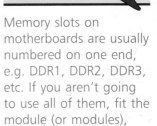

Hot tip

Memory slots on motherboards are usually numbered on one end, e.g. DDR1, DDR2, DDR3, etc. If you aren't going to use all of them, fit the module (or modules), in the lowest numbered slots.

2 Align the cut-out on the module pin connector with the engaging lug on the slot

...cont'd

Beware

If you find yourself trying to force the module retaining clips to close, stop immediately. Either the module is not fully inserted or you are using the wrong type. In this situation, all you are likely to do is break the clips or damage the motherboard.

3 Press down on both ends. You may need to exert some firm pressure here

4 When the module is correctly seated, the retaining clips will close automatically

(4) Motherboards

This chapter gives you the low-down on the most important board in the PC. Every part of the system is affected by the motherboard, so you can't afford any mistakes here. Read on to discover the available types and what you will need in terms of features and specifications.

BIOS chip

PCI socket

PCI-Express socket

SATA drive sockets

Floppy drive socket

USB connectors

Battery

ATA hard drive socket

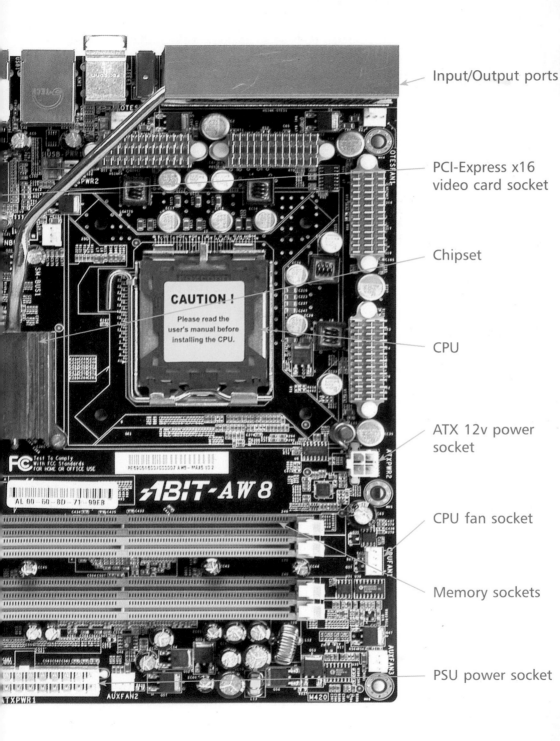

Input/Output ports

PCI-Express x16
video card socket

Chipset

CPU

ATX 12v power
socket

CPU fan socket

Memory sockets

PSU power socket

Overview

Using the human body as an analogy, if the CPU is the brain of a computer, then the motherboard is its central nervous system. Every single part of a computer system is connected, either directly or indirectly, to this piece of circuitry. This makes it the most important circuit board in the system.

Because of this, deciding which board to buy will be an important decision. Not only do you have to consider the features and quality of the board itself, you also have to think about how it will affect the other parts of the system.

Before we get into what you should be looking for in a motherboard, lets have a brief look at the more important of its functions.

- CPU and RAM – the motherboard provides sockets which enable these devices to be connected to the system

- BUSs – these are basically "roads" and provide routes for the relaying of data

- Chipset – this device is the interface between the system and the CPU. It organizes and controls everything in the computer, and is an extremely important component

- Drive sockets – these allow hard, floppy and CD/DVD drives to be connected to the system

- Expansion slots – these enable a system to be expanded by the addition of extra devices, such as video cards, modems, and sound cards

- Integration – many boards come with integrated sound and video systems. Other functions that may be supplied include network adapters, modems, hardware firewalls, and RAID hard drive controllers

- BIOS – this chip controls a computer's boot-up routines and provides settings for some of the system's components

- Ports – these are found at the back of the board, and provide a means of connecting peripheral devices such as printers, keyboards and mice

Hot tip

The Internet is a mine of useful information regarding motherboards. There are many sites that specialize in benchmark testing of new motherboards as they are released. These tests quickly identify a board's relative strengths and weaknesses. The reviews on these sites are well worth reading.

Hot tip

There are dozens of companies involved in the manufacture of motherboards, and as with most products, whatever their nature, it usually pays in the long run to buy from a reputable and established company.

Buying a Motherboard

Before you can make a decision on which motherboard to buy, you must already have made some decisions regarding the components you intend to install in it, i.e. the CPU and memory, and the interfaces that your devices are going to use, e.g. ATA, SATA, PCI-Express, etc.

Don't forget

AMD and Intel CPUs use completely different types of socket. They are not interchangeable – an Intel CPU will not fit into a motherboard designed for an AMD CPU and vice versa.

There are quite a few other factors to be considered as well. We'll start with the CPU.

Central Processing Unit (CPU)

The first consideration with the CPU is physical compatibility with the motherboard. This means that the board must have the socket that the CPU is designed to use.

A quick look at the specifications will ensure you get this right. The CPU specifications will specify the socket required – socket 478, 939, LGA775, etc. The motherboard specifications will specify the socket provided. They will also tell you which CPUs the board is designed for – you really can't go wrong.

The next consideration is the motherboard's FSB. Ideally, it will be the same as the CPU's FSB. However, it's not critical if it isn't. The system will still work but at the lower of the two speeds (see page 50 for more on this). Again, you need to look at the specifications.

Beware

Windows XP and Windows Vista both incorporate some technologies and features that must be supported by the motherboard in order for them to work. While older motherboards may well be available at knockdown prices to enable the retailer to shift old stock, and thus be tempting for budget conscious buyers, they may end up with systems that does not get the best out of these operating systems.

...cont'd

Hot tip

The most foolproof method of matching the CPU to the motherboard is by using the CPU manufacturers' system-building guides. Simply key in the required information and you will see which motherboards will be compatible with the chosen CPU.

Check that the board provides full support for the features and requirements of the CPU. Just because it has the right socket is no guarantee of this. For example, if you go for an Intel CPU that incorporates Hyper-Threading technology, you must get a board that supports Hyper-Threading.

Finally, check that the board can support the clock speed of the CPU – don't confuse this with FSB.

A good method of ensuring you get the correct motherboard for your CPU is to go to the CPU manufacturer's website. For example, at AMD's site (www.amd.com) you will find a system-building guide, as shown below:

1 Select your CPU

2 Select your system's form factor

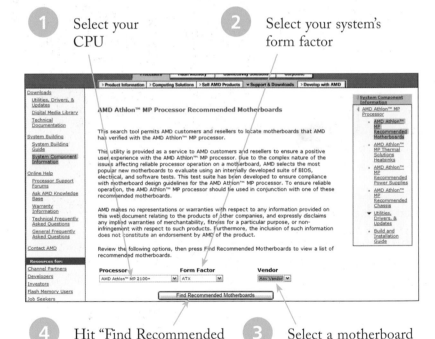

4 Hit "Find Recommended Motherboards"

3 Select a motherboard manufacturer

You will now be presented with a list of motherboards that are compatible with your chosen CPU.

Intel (www.intel.com) have a similar facility.

Memory (RAM)

There are three things you need to consider with relation to motherboards and RAM.

1) Can the board fully utilize the amount of RAM installed?

2) Does the board support the rated speed of the RAM?

3) Will the RAM modules physically fit on the board?

With regard to the amount of RAM, most motherboards of even half-decent quality will be able to support at least 1 GB, while many will support 2, or even 4 GB. As few people are going to need any more than 1 GB, in most cases it should not be an issue.

As far as speed is concerned, ideally the memory's FSB will be equal to the motherboard's FSB. It is not critical though, if it isn't.

For example, if you put a stick of high-speed PC2-8000 DDR2 RAM, which runs at at 1000 MHz into a motherboard that only supports 800 MHz, the system will still work. However, the RAM will operate at the lower speed so you will not be getting the best out of it.

Unless you are reusing an old motherboard or memory module, you will have no problems fitting your RAM into the board. Most RAM modules now are DDR 184-pin DIMMs, and virtually all mainstream motherboards will accept these. If you are using 240-pin DDR2 modules, you will need a motherboard designed to accept these.

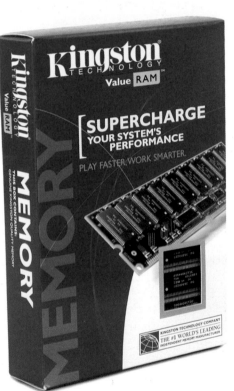

Hot tip

Present 32-bit systems can use a maximum of 4 GB of memory. 64-bit systems can use up to 16,000,000 GB (theoretically). In practice though, the first 64-bit motherboards are initially offering four DIMM slots, and as the maximum size of a DIMM module is currently 2 GB, the maximum you can install on these boards is 8 GB.

However, as most home-systems use no more than 512 MB of memory, 8 GB is still an enormous amount.

Don't forget

If you intend to build a power-system that uses a large amount of memory, make sure the motherboard you buy is capable of utilizing it all.

In addition, if you are going to use the latest DDR2 memory, this must also be supported by the motherboard and CPU.

...cont'd

Don't forget

A motherboard's quality and performance is directly proportional to that of the chipset. Among other functions carried out by this device are the board's integrated video and sound systems.

Chipset

A chipset is an integrated circuit on the motherboard that controls the flow of data to and from key components of the PC. These include the CPU, memory, the BIOS and devices connected to the system's buses, e.g. PCI and PCI-Express, ATA drive and AGP sockets.

It also provides a motherboard's integrated functions, such as video and sound systems. The amount and type of RAM that the board can handle is also determined by the chipset.

So to a very large degree, the chipset dictates the quality and features of the motherboard. Essentially, when you look at a motherboard's specifications, you are looking at the chipset's specifications.

The major players in this particular market are Intel, Via and SIS, and to a lesser degree, AMD and Nvidia. Go with any of these manufacturers and you won't be far wrong. However, chipsets from Intel are generally reckoned to be the best and these are the ones we recommend. Note that this will probably mean going for an Intel system as Intel chipsets are usually found on motherboards built to take Intel CPUs.

Front Side Bus (FSB)

The FSB is the speed at which the motherboard communicates with the rest of the system and is also known as the External Clock Speed.

When choosing the board, you must ensure that its FSB matches the FSB of certainly the CPU, and ideally, the memory module/s as well. If it doesn't, the performance of these components, and hence the system, will be degraded.

Modern motherboards provide several different FSBs and will automatically configure (synchronize) themselves to run at the FSB of the CPU.

Sockets

The motherboard's sockets allow you to expand and update your system as and when required. For this reason, it is important that your chosen board has the right type and also enough of them.

PCI

Currently, this is the standard interface for internal hardware devices. The only thing you need to check here is that the board supplies enough sockets for your devices. Most provide four or five but there are some that have only one or two, so check it out.

PCI-Express

This is an enhanced version of the PCI interface that provides much better performance and it is expected to eventually supersede PCI. To make use of it, you will have to replace your existing PCI devices with PCI-Express versions. If you are not prepared to do this yet, we recommend that you still buy a PCI-Express enabled motherboard as, currently, they also provide PCI sockets for backward compatibility. So when you are ready to make the switch, you won't also have to buy a new motherboard.

AGP

This socket is provided for AGP video cards. If you have, or intend to get, one of these cards, make sure the motherboard has an AGP socket (not all do). Also, AGP comes in various speeds – 1x, 2x, 4x and 8x. Make sure the board supports the AGP speed used by your video card.

Note that the PCI-Express interface also provides a socket (x16) for video cards. Many of the top-end video cards are now using this, so if hardcore gaming is your forte, you may want to make sure that your motherboard has a x16 PCI-Express socket.

Drive

The current standard interface for connecting drive units to the system is ATA and all motherboards provide this. However, the newer SATA interface (see pages 111-112), which provides many advantages, is rapidly taking over.

So even if you are planning to use an ATA drive in your new system, it makes sense to buy a SATA enabled board as they also provide ATA sockets for backward compatibility. When your ATA drive eventually dies, you can then replace it with a SATA model.

Hot tip

Even if you currently have no PCI-Express devices or a SATA drive, by buying a motherboard equipped with these technologies, your system will be future-proofed.

Hot tip

If you intend to buy an AGP video card, make sure the motherboard has an AGP slot. Not all do, so it's worth checking out.

Form Factors

As with other components, the size, and installation parameters of a motherboard are specified by its form factor. The one currently in vogue is the ATX standard.

Variations of ATX include Mini-ATX and Micro-ATX. These are scaled down versions that are used in smaller system cases. While Mini- and Micro-ATX boards are perfectly functional, they do provide fewer PCI sockets, which limits your options regarding add-on devices.

So unless you intend to build a PC that is physically small, we recommend a full size ATX motherboard.

Another option that may be attractive for those building a high-performance system is the BTX standard. Introduced in 2004, this has been designed primarily to deal with the large amount of heat produced by today's top-end CPUs and video cards.

A BTX system employs a thermal module that has a single fan and heatsink, plus an optimized design for airflow that eliminates the need for several case fans.

Integrated Hardware

All motherboards come with built-in hardware, typically sound and video systems. Until fairly recently, however, neither of these has offered much in the way of quality and features. For example, early video did not have 3D capability, which is essential for playing 3D games and the sound systems could only handle the two little speakers that manufacturers typically supplied.

Today, the situation is much different. The sound systems now supplied with motherboards can support multiple-speaker setups, and the video systems have full 3D capabilities.

For most users, these systems are perfectly adequate for the more mundane and undemanding computer tasks, such as word-processing, email and even the occasional game as long as you don't expect top-notch performance from it.

Note that while nearly all motherboards provide integrated sound, many do not provide integrated video. So if this is something that you require, be sure to check that the board includes it.

Quite apart from sound and video, current motherboards also offer a range of other hardware, such as modems, RAID controllers and network controllers. These represent a considerable cost saving over buying stand-alone devices. Another advantage is that your expansion options are increased as you will have spare expansion card sockets that would otherwise be occupied.

Ports

A computer's ports are the assortment of sockets situated at the top-right at the rear of the system case. These allow you to connect peripheral devices, such as printers, scanners and modems.

Most of the ports are standard and are provided with the majority of motherboards. A typical example is shown below:

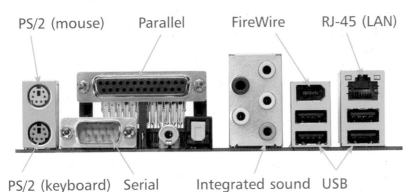

Hot tip

Go for a motherboard with as many USB ports as possible, as virtually all peripherals now use the USB interface. This has considerable advantages over the older PS/2 and Parallel Port methods of connection.

Also, make sure you get USB 2; this is some forty times faster than USB 1.

The USB ports are the most important ones. While virtually all motherboards supply them (usually four), some boards will give you six, or even eight, and with the current dominance of USB as a means of connecting peripheral devices, the more of these you have the better.

While on the subject of USB, this comes in two standards – USB 1 and USB 2. The difference between the two is data transfer speed; USB 1 has a transfer rate of 12 MB/s, while USB 2 transfers at 480 MB/s.

The latter is considerably faster and will make an appreciable difference to operations such as scanning and downloading photos and video from digital cameras. Current motherboards provide USB 2, so make sure you aren't fobbed-off with an outdated board that only provides USB 1.

Hot tip

The Serial and Parallel ports used to provide the main method of connecting peripheral devices to a PC. With the advent of USB, however, they are now virtually redundant. Motherboard manufacturers still supply them for backward compatibility, though.

53

Types of Motherboard

Dual-Processor Motherboards

A dual-processor motherboard has two CPU sockets, which allows two separate CPUs to be installed. These act independently of each other and have their own hardware support (as opposed to a dual-core CPU, where the system's hardware is shared).

The result, not surprisingly, is a huge boost in processing power. However, this type of setup is only going to be required by those who multi-task with CPU intensive applications. It does come at a price as well – an expensive dual CPU motherboard, plus two CPUs. The typical home user has no need for such a system.

Dual-Channel Motherboards

Traditionally, motherboards have provided just one memory channel, which usually results in the system's memory having insufficient bandwidth to keep pace with the CPU, thus creating a performance bottleneck.

Dual-channel motherboards provide a second parallel channel, which effectively doubles the bandwidth available to the memory. With two channels working simultaneously, the bottleneck can be reduced to a certain degree. Rather than wait for memory technology to improve, dual-channel architecture takes the existing technology and enhances the way it is utilized.

Dual-Video Card Motherboards

For the ultimate in graphics performance, the two main graphics chip manufacturers, ATI and Nvidia, both provide a dual-video card setup. Nvidia's is called SLI (Scalable Link Interface) and ATI's is known as CrossFire.

These employ matched pairs of video cards that operate in tandem to produce vastly improved 3D graphics performance. Their main use, not surprisingly, is hardcore gaming. The frame rate in certain games can be doubled, while the games can be run at higher, more detailed resolutions, without loss of performance.

The catch of course is the cost. Both systems require two of the latest PCI-Express video cards and a CrossFire or SLI enabled motherboard equipped with two x16 PCI-Express sockets. Furthermore, as these systems are only as good as the weakest link in the chain, you will also need a top-end CPU, and at least 1 GB of high-performance DDR (ideally DDR 2) memory.

Hot tip

Dual-channel motherboards provide color-coded pairs of memory sockets. In each pair, you must install two identical modules, otherwise the system will default to single-channel mode.

Beware

Not all games will benefit from a CrossFire or SLI setup, as the graphics engines used by many of them are not designed for use with a multiple-graphics core. They will no doubt show an improvement but not enough to justify the high cost of the setup. However, most recent games will benefit.

Installing a Motherboard

Your system case may come with a sliding or removable side panel on which to attach the motherboard. The case we are using here does not, however, the procedure is the same.

The first thing to do is locate the plastic bag inside the case that will contain various fixings and rubber feet for the case to stand on. In this bag, you will find seven or eight brass stand-offs to which the motherboard will be screwed. Put these to one side. At this stage you may as well fit the rubber feet to the bottom of the case; it's easier to do it now when the case is empty.

Next, you need to remove the Input/Output shield from the rear of the case, as shown below.

Hot tip

The advantage of a sliding or removable side panel is when the motherboard has to be accessed, or removed from the system for some reason. Without one, you may have to first remove the PSU and disconnect all the drive unit cables.

1. Remove the retaining screws

2. Remove the cover

Hot tip

The Input/Output shield is there to prevent you from inadvertently poking things through, which can touch and maybe damage the motherboard. It can also prevent your inquisitive kids from getting an electric shock.

...cont'd

Beware

Make sure you screw in a stand-off to support the motherboard at each corner, plus two in the middle. If you don't, when you come to install your expansion cards and connect the drive cables, the board will flex. This can easily break a circuit and trash the board.

Now you need to establish exactly where to place the brass stand-offs. The side panel will have numerous threaded holes, combinations of which will accept motherboards of differing dimensions. Holding the board in place will reveal the ones you want. Screw the stand-offs into these holes. You can do this with your fingers and then tighten them up with a suitable spanner or a pair of pliers.

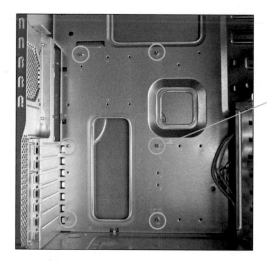

3 Stand-offs screwed in place ready for the motherboard

4 Using the supplied screws, screw the motherboard into place. Don't overtighten them – this is a PC you're assembling, not a car engine

Hot tip

When screwing the motherboard down, make sure that you use the screws supplied for the purpose. If you use screws from some other source and the heads are oversized, you could short-circuit the board.

Finally, you must refit the Input/ Output shield. If the one supplied with the case lines up with the motherboard's ports, then use it. You may, however, find that it does not, in which case you will have to use the one supplied with the motherboard. These are usually somewhat flimsy, but adequate, affairs that clip into place from the inside.

5 System Cases

A well designed system case will make a significant contribution to the performance of the PC. We look at what's available in the case market, and consider the features and specifications that will influence your choice of case.

Types of Case

The case is where all the main components of the PC go and is a much underrated part of the system. Apart from protecting the components from the outside world, a well designed case will help to maintain a safe and stable operating temperature; this is crucial for the reliability of a system.

Computer cases come in two main types – Desktop and Tower.

Desktop Cases

These are the smallest and are often used with the monitor sitting on top. This provides their only real advantage – the relatively small amount of desktop space the system occupies.

The downside is that they provide limited potential for expansion (typically, having only two external drive bays and one internal drive bay), are awkward to work in and can be difficult to keep adequately cooled.

Tower Cases

Tower cases are by far the most common due to the extra internal space they offer. Not only does this allow more components to be installed, but it is also easier to keep them cool due to better airflow characteristics.

Towers come in three main sizes – Mini, Mid and Full.

Mini-towers are similar in volume to desktop cases, but due to their design, are generally easier to work in and have more capacity.

A full-tower case is the largest size available and provides the most flexibility with room for a large number of drives and other devices.

Mid-towers are a compromise between mini- and full-towers and are the ones found in most home-PC systems.

Note that tower cases are often supplied with an integral power supply unit, which can make them appear to be a bargain.

However, these PSUs tend to be low-quality affairs and our recommendation is to avoid them. Instead, buy your case and PSU separately.

Gaming Cases

These are tower cases, but as with all things to do with PC gaming, they are a cut above the average. They provide two important features required in a gaming system – efficient heat dispersal and looks (aesthetics).

This type of system requires high-end CPUs and video cards, both of which produce serious amounts of heat.

Gaming cases are built to get rid of this by using anodized aluminum (this has better heat transfer characteristics than the steel used in cheaper cases) for the case itself and an optimized design that maximizes the cooling effect of airflow within the case.

We'll look at the issue of case aesthetics on pages 64-66.

Important Case Features

Capacity

The case needs to have enough space in which to accommodate all your devices, ideally without cramming them in (this can lead to over-heating). If you only need room for one hard drive, one CD/DVD drive and a floppy drive and have no intentions of ever adding more, a desktop case will be adequate.

More than this will require a mini-tower, which can have room for up to five external drives and four internal drives. Very few people are going to need more capacity than this. However, minitowers provide little leg room, and so can be awkward to work in.

Therefore, a mid-tower is the option recommended as it provides all the capacity you are ever likely to need, is easy to work in, and is not overly obtrusive.

Don't forget

Something to consider if you are thinking small is that desktop and mini-cases provide very little in the way of maneuverability when it comes to installing the various parts. This can turn a relatively straightforward exercise into something much more difficult.

BTX systems employ a specially designed cooling module that increases airflow threefold in comparison to a standard ATX system. Furthermore, as the cooling system is so effective, the fan it uses can run up to 40 per cent slower than in ATX systems. This results in much reduced noise levels.

60

Form Factors

System cases are built to form factors that enable them be correctly matched with the motherboard and power supply unit. This ensures that these devices will be physically compatible.

ATX is the current form factor and the vast majority of motherboards, power supply units and system cases are designed to this standard. Unless you want a small system, in which case you will look at Mini-ATX and Micro-ATX cases, an ATX case is almost certainly what will be required.

If you intend to build a high-performance, or silent, system, there is the BTX form factor to consider. This relatively new standard (introduced in 2004) is designed to cope with the main problems faced by this type of system – large amounts of heat, and the noise produced by the fans required to disperse the heat – see margin note.

However, there are issues with BTX. First, it requires a BTX motherboard – you cannot use an ATX board in a BTX case. Second, its reception by the PC industry has been lukewarm to say the least. As a result, there are relatively few BTX cases and motherboards on the market, which means that you will be severely restricted in terms of choice.

Cooling

All the system's components are designed to operate within specific heat tolerances, and if they do, you will have no problems.

If your system overheats though, and remember, you won't get any warning messages flash up on your screen, your parts may fail months or even years before they should do. It will also be unstable and prone to inexplicable crashes and errors.

Fortunately, for most users, over-heating isn't going to be an issue – the average home-PC, which typically, will have a low-end or mid-range CPU, a modem, a hard drive, a CD/DVD drive and maybe one or two other devices, will be cooled quite adequately by the PSU and CPU fans.

However, if you are intent on a more sophisticated system that will include additional or high-performance devices, each of which will increase the temperature within the case, then extra cooling may well be required. Here you have several options.

The simplest is to buy a case that has an integral fan to increase airflow. Another is a BTX system. A gaming case (see page 59) is a third option. For really efficient cooling, you can go for a water-cooled system; these work on the same principle as house central heating systems.

If you decide to go this route, the simplest option is to buy a case with the cooling system pre-installed. Many case manufacturers, such as Koolance and Thermaltake, provide these.

Also available are water-cooling kits, which can be fitted by the user in most system cases. These comprise a radiator, tubing,

waterblocks (to transfer heat from the components to the coolant) and a pump. Most kits also incorporate a fan.

Installation is straightforward with the largest component, the radiator, usually fixed outside to the top of the case. Waterblocks are provided for the main heat producing parts (CPU, motherboard chipset, and the video card) and are simply fixed to the top of the device (a Koolance waterblock fitted to a video card is shown above).

Noise

The downside of cooling is the noise produced by the fans. Single CPU, PSU and case fans are not too bad but a combination of them, and the ones used on video cards, can be very noisy. To overcome this you have several options:

The first is so-called silent fans. Note that we have yet to see one that is truly silent, but they are quieter than standard fans. These are available for CPUs, video cards and system cases.

Also available are temperature regulated fans or a separate fan controller (see margin note). These adjust the fan speed automatically by monitoring the case temperature. The advantage is that the fans will be running at maximum speed (and thus noise levels) only when necessary, i.e. when the PC is heavily loaded.

Beware

A drawback with most water cooled systems is increased noise levels as they usually incorporate at least one fan, not to mention an electric pump. However, there are some that are available with no fans such as the Zalman Reserator.

There can also be problems with airlocks, which will need bleeding as with a central heating system. Also, be aware that cheaper systems may not include all the necessary parts – typically the fan/s.

Hot tip

If you do buy a fan controller, make sure it features a temperature monitoring function. This will tell you whether the fans are sufficiently cooling the system. If the computer's internal temperature reaches a critical point, an alarm is triggered in the form of a beep tone, or flashing LED, to signal that the system is overheating.

...cont'd

Alternatively, you can get manual controllers, which allow you to manually control the speed, and thus the noise levels, of up to four separate fans.

Good quality power supply units come with automatically regulated fans, the speed of which are controlled by the load placed on the PSU. These provide another option for minimizing noise.

A different method is to soundproof the case. As with cooling systems, you can buy cases that are already soundproofed, or do the soundproofing yourself with a proprietary kit.

Many of the sound-proofed cases currently available are popular models from selected manufacturers that have been adapted by firms specializing in sound-proofing. They are expensive, though.

The kits are a much cheaper option. They take the form of self-adhesive mats (shown above) that you cut to size and then fix in place. Something to be aware of here, is that these mats can be anything up to twenty millimeters in thickness and can considerably reduce the internal dimensions of the case. Even in a mid-tower, you may well have difficulty in fitting the PC's components afterwards. In a mini or desktop case, maybe not at all.

Yet another option is to use specialized heatsinks. These are available from manufacturers such as Zalman, and are weird and wonderful creations of copper and aluminum that provide a much larger surface area to dissipate the unwanted heat.

Hot tip

If you use one of these heatsinks without a fan, make sure that you check the device's operating temperature. In the case of CPUs (and sometimes video cards), this can be done in the system's BIOS program.

These can be used to replace low-end and mid-range CPU and video card fans completely, or in conjunction with smaller, lower speed, and thus quieter fans.

Note that high-performance CPUs and video cards will still need a fan as well, but lower specification devices will be adequately cooled by one of these heatsinks.

Construction

Many of the cheaper models use thin, low-grade steel, which results in a flimsy case with poor heat transfer characteristics. With these you may also find that edges are not deburred, with the result that you may cut or scratch yourself.

Other, typical, problems include poorly threaded and/or misaligned screw holes, which makes device installation difficult, LEDs that burn out after a few hours of use, and low-quality switches that soon fail or push right into the front panel making it difficult, or impossible, to access them.

Good quality cases are constructed of thicker, higher-grade steel, and high-end models are made of anodized aluminum, which is not only much lighter but also much more efficient at heat dispersement. Many of them also use thumbscrews for quick access to the inside of the case and snap-in fastening methods that make device installation much easier.

A very useful feature for the self-builder found on some cases, is a removable or slide-out tray. These are particularly handy for accessing motherboards that would otherwise require other parts to be removed first.

You might also consider buying a case with a door that covers the front panel. This will considerably reduce the amount of dust that, over time, will infiltrate your CD/DVD drive unit's internal mechanism. Some are lockable, which provides an extra security option. For an added touch of luxury, you can get even cases where the door is motorized.

Some cases also provide a front panel digital readout of the internal case temperature as shown on the right.

Ports

Traditionally, a computer's ports have all been located at the rear of the case where they are not easily accessible. Many cases these days supply USB (usually two), microphone, and speaker connections, on the case's front panel. These can be very useful for the temporary connection of a digital camera and a digital video camera.

Hot tip

If you do buy a cheap case that includes an integral PSU, our advice is to replace it with a good quality model.

Some of these devices are truly awful and will cause you a lot of problems.

63

Hot tip

If you use a digital camera, you will find it extremely handy to have a USB port at the front of the case.

Aesthetics

When PCs first hit the streets, they all came in a rather bland beige rectangular box. While perfectly functional, they didn't exactly set the pulse racing. PCs bought from the large manufacturers still tend to follow this trend.

Nowadays, however, there are a huge range of cases in all colors and many different styles. These allow the self-builder to have a computer that is a bit more interesting visually.

If you investigate this end of the market, you will find cases in brushed aluminum, clear and translucent acrylic, with transparent side panels, and some with glowing LEDs that illuminate the case making it glow like a demon's eyes.

Apart from looks, you will also get high-quality construction, usually in anodized aluminum, which as we have already mentioned, is more efficient than steel at heat dispersement.

However, while these cases are stylish and attractive, they are very expensive when compared to standard cases – some of them will cost nearly as much as the parts inside them.

There are available though, many stylish enough cases at a reasonable price, as long as you are prepared to accept a lesser quality of construction.

Beware

Computer style comes at a significant cost. Expect to have to dig deep, if looks, combined with quality are important to you.

Case Modding

An increasingly common feature found on modern system cases is the transparent side panel, or window.

However, having the guts of the PC on view requires something interesting to see, and this provides a perfect opportunity for customization.

This is known as case modding and it is now extremely popular – people even take their PCs to modding conventions.

So, if you are looking to make a statement with your PC and can't find anything off the shelf that appeals, you will find a multitude of products that enable you to do the job yourself.

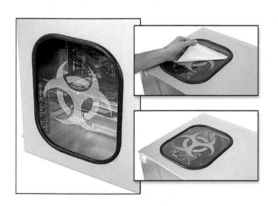

The first place to start is the transparent side panel. Instead of settling for a plain acrylic window, there are a wide range of window decals available with which to jazz it up.

Some, like the example shown above, are simple designs, while others are more complex or ultraviolet reactive, which produces a glowing pattern when illuminated.

Next, you will need to fit a source of ultraviolet light inside the PC.

...cont'd

Hot tip

At the risk of taking things to extremes, you can even get UV reactive cable ties.

The standard for PC lighting is cold cathode, a type of ultra-violet fluorescent light that's five times brighter than neon. It is available in many colors, and has the great advantage of not producing heat, a fact that makes it ideal for use with PCs. Just fix the unit in place and then connect it to the PSU (not forgetting to put the sunglasses on first).

Those of you who are really keen can add colored lighting to literally every component in the case. To begin with, all the fans – CPU, video card, and system case – can be replaced by LED or cold cathode versions. Even the fan grilles can be replaced with customized grilles of various designs.

The ATA/SATA drive cables can be replaced with ultraviolet reactive cables. The memory modules can have flashing neon strips fitted at the top.

PSUs are usually dull and uninteresting – buck the trend and go for a model with an attractive case, LED fans, and UV reactive cabling. It won't be cheap but it'll certainly look the business.

If you still can't see clearly, you can add even more lights to the outside of the case. For example, the feet can be replaced with illuminated versions.

By the time you've finished, the computer will be lit up like the Vegas Strip at night. We suspect the novelty may soon wear off but it will be fun doing it. Nor does it cost a great deal.

6

Power Supply Units (PSU)

Power supply units are much underrated components and the wrong purchase can prove to be a very costly mistake. This chapter explains why, and shows you the specifications that need to be considered when buying a PSU.

Overview

Power supply units are one of the least interesting components in a computer system, but a good one is absolutely essential for a PC to perform reliably. They are also the part most likely to fail and, when they do, they have a nasty habit of taking other components with them, RAM modules and CPUs in particular.

For these reasons, the PSU is not a component to economize on – if you do, it could cost you dearly in the long run.

Specifications

Specifications you need to consider when buying a PSU are:

Power Rating
PSUs are rated in watts (W) and, as far as desktop PCs are concerned, range from 300 W to about 500 W. Which one you will need depends on the total amount of power required by the parts in your system. The following is a guide:

- Mini-tower or Desktop – 300 to 350 W
- Mid-tower – 350 to 400 W
- Full-tower – 400 to 500 W

However, bear in mind this is a rough guide and doesn't take into account the power requirements of high-end CPUs and video cards (these two components are the most power hungry devices in a computer system).

Beware

A high quality power supply unit will be one of the most important purchases you make. Trying to save a few dollars here could cost you several hundred further down the line.

Hot tip

The power supply unit you buy must be rated in excess of the combined wattage ratings of all the system's components. However, unless you are building a high-powered system with one of the latest processors and video cards, the figures in the guide opposite will be adequate in most cases.

A more accurate way of determining what you need is to refer to the following table:

Component	Power Required
High-end video card	120 W
Mid-range video card	60 W
Low-end video card	30 W
High-end CPU	110 W
Mid-range CPU	60 W
Low-end CPU	40 W
Motherboard	35 W
DDR SDRAM module	7 W
DDR2 SDRAM module	15 W
ATA hard drive	15 W
SATA hard drive	13 W
SCSI hard drive	40 W
Optical drive	25 W
Floppy drive	5 W
80 mm cooling fan	2 W
Expansion cards (including sound)	5 W
Fan controller	10 W
USB device	3 W
FireWire device	8 W
Zip drive	10 W

Beware

Do not judge the quality of a PSU purely by its wattage rating. This is a common mistake, similar to rating speakers by wattage.

69

This shows the maximum power (approximately) needed for all the individual parts in a computer system. It will enable you to work out with a good degree of accuracy what PSU your system will need in terms of wattage. Whatever figure you come up with, get a PSU of a higher rating. For example, if you calculate that you will need a 350 W PSU, get one rated at 400 W. There are two reasons for doing this.

First, PSUs work best with a bit in hand. Running one at full load is not recommended if you want it to last any length of time. Second, if you decide later to add an extra device to your system, you will have enough power available to run it.

Don't forget

It is important to get a PSU that will handle your system's power requirements and still have a bit to spare. This gives you the option to expand the system in the future without also having to buy a more powerful PSU.

Overload Protection

Good quality PSUs incorporate circuitry that will prevent damage to other components in the system, should they fail. These circuits monitor the voltage, current and heat levels of the PSU. If any of these exceed a designated limit, the PSU will automatically shutdown, rather than blowing as cheap models will.

This is an extremely important feature as all PSUs, no matter how good, will eventually fail. If they blow, they are quite likely to take other components with them – most commonly the motherboard, memory modules, and CPU.

Good PSUs also offer protection against voltage surges in the external AC supply.

Cheap PSUs do not offer any protection and so should be avoided. The output voltages of these units also tend to fluctuate, particularly under heavy loads. This can be the cause of general system instability such as crashes and sudden reboots.

So when making your choice, check the specifications and make sure they include protection circuitry.

Form Factor

All power supply units conform to a form factor. You must ensure that the form factor of the PSU you buy matches that of the system case and motherboard. If you are using a mid- or full-tower case, you will need a full-size ATX PSU. If you are using a micro-ATX case, you will need an SFX/micro-ATX PSU.

Cooling

A good PSU will not only keep itself cool, it will help to cool the other components in the case as well.

All PSUs have a rear mounted fan that draws cool air in from the front of the case and expels heat from the back.

Better models will also have an under or side mounted fan (shown left), which will kick in when the PSU is highly loaded. This provides extra cooling when it is needed and can also extend the working life of the PSU considerably.

Beware

It is essential to make sure your chosen PSU incorporates protection circuitry that will shut it down when problems occur. Otherwise, it will eventually blow and you may well lose many of the other parts in the system as well.

Connectors

All PSUs supply 12 volt molex connectors, which are used to power devices such as CD/DVD drives, hard drives and case fans. Check that the power supply unit provides enough of these connectors to power all the devices that you intend to install.

The recent SATA hard drives and PCI-Express video cards use connectors that are not supplied with standard ATX PSUs. If you plan to use either of these, get a PSU built to the more recent ATX V2.0 or V2.1 standards, both of which supply them.

Note that it is possible to use a SATA drive with a standard ATX PSU but you will need an adapter on one of the molex connectors. This will leave you a molex connector short and so you may not have enough of them for the other devices.

Weight

It is a little known fact that the quality of a PSU is directly proportional to its weight. This provides a quick and easy way of evaluating these devices.

A heavy PSU has larger and more capacitors, thicker wires, a larger transformer, larger heat sinks and more connectors than a light one. All of these factors are crucial with regard to the quality of the device.

This specification, typically, won't be shown by PC component vendors. However, it should be available at the manufacturer's website.

Efficiency

The efficiency of a PSU is determined by the ratio of power going into it, compared to the power coming out (the difference is the amount of power converted to heat by the device).

This is an important specification because the less efficient the PSU, the greater the amount of power it will convert to heat. This raises the operating temperature not only of the PSU's components, but also the PC's. The long-term effect will be a reduction in the PSU's, and possibly the PC's, working life.

Efficiency is expressed in percentile, and you should look for a figure no less than 65 per cent. High-quality PSUs will have an efficiency rating nearer 85 per cent.

Hot tip

Even if you aren't installing any in your new system, buy a PSU that provides connections for SATA hard drives and PCI-Express expansion cards. This will save you from having to mess around with adapters when you do.

Don't forget

The weight of a PSU is a very good indicator of it's quality.

Hot tip

A welcome side-effect of a high efficiency rating is less noise. The cooler the PSU, the slower and thus less noisy, its fan/s have to run.

External AC Power Supply

You should also consider the AC supply to your PC. The vast majority of people never give this a thought – it's always there, it always works, so what's there to think about?

Well, actually, quite a lot. AC power supplies suffer from a range of faults, which can, and do, cause problems with PCs. These include:

- Blackouts
- Line noise
- Power surges (spikes)
- Over voltage
- Frequency variation

There are others but these are the ones which most affect a PC. Power surges can cause damage and, in worst case scenarios such as lightening storms, may fry a PC completely.

Usually though, you won't even be aware of them as, typically, they have a duration of less than 0.001 seconds. They do, however, cause PCs to lock-up and crash. Furthermore, voltage spikes have a cumulative effect and over time will cause components to fail well before they should do.

To eliminate these problems, the following devices are available:

- Surge Suppressors
- Power Conditioners
- Uninterruptible Power Supplies

Surge Suppressors

A surge suppressor (shown right) smooths out any momentary increases in the supply voltage, thus ensuring that the input to the PC's PSU is at a constant level.

Courtesy of Belkin Corporation

As with all your PC's components, it pays to investigate a surge suppressor's specifications before handing over the cash. For example, a good model will also be capable of removing line noise and distortion in the AC signal, thus delivering a "clean" supply.

Hot tip

Power surges are also commonplace on telephone lines. Apart from breaking a dial-up Internet connection, they can also damage the modem. Consider buying a telephone line surge protector.

Beware

In the event of a close proximity lightening storm, switch the computer off and disconnect it from the AC supply. Otherwise, you may end up with a pile of charred plastic and silicon.

72

Surge suppressor protection is rated in Joules; this being the amount of energy that the device is designed to handle. The higher the number, the better the level of protection.

A figure of 500 to 600 Joules will provide adequate protection for the home user.

Power or Line Conditioners

These devices work by filtering the signal to eliminate electrical interference that can cause noise. They also provide voltage surge protection and are a step up from surge suppressors.

Courtesy of Belkin Corporation

This is due to the more efficient way they clean up the AC signal. Not surprisingly, however, they cost more and can also be quite bulky in size.

Uninterruptible Power Supply Units (UPS)

These provide the best form of protection and are commonly found in office and corporate environments where data protection is critical.

Apart from surge suppression and power conditioning capabilities, they also have a battery that will maintain power to the computer system in the event of a power cut. This allows ample time to save work in progress and close systems down correctly.

Courtesy of Belkin Corporation

For home users, a good surge suppressor that also has line conditioning capabilities is the device to go for.

Beware

Don't underestimate the adverse effects a dirty or fluctuating AC supply can have on your computer. The way to protect against this is with an appropriate surge protector or line conditioner.

Don't forget

If you do mission-critical work on your PC, or it must be available at all times, you need to invest in an Uninterruptible Power Supply unit.

This device will provide several hours worth of backup power.

Installing a PSU

1 Slide the PSU into position

The PSU supplies four different connectors. These are:

Motherboard Power

CD/Hard Drive Power

Floppy Drive Power

ATX 12V

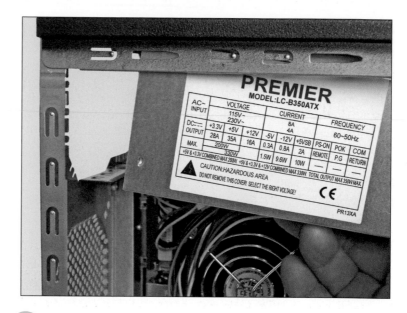

2 Supporting the PSU at the front, screw it to the rear of the case with the supplied screws

3 From the jumble of PSU connectors, disentangle the largest one. This is the power supply for the motherboard

4 Locate the motherboard's power socket (see pages 44-45) and plug in the supply from the PSU

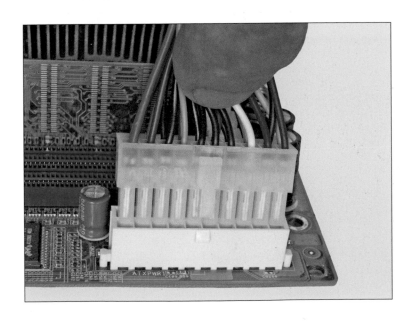

Beware

When sliding the power supply unit into position, take care not to make contact with the motherboard.

Don't forget

When you have installed the power supply unit, remember to check that the voltage selector at the back (if there is one) is set correctly. Also, make sure that the PSU's on/off switch (also at the back) is in the "on" position.

Case Connections

1 Finally, connect all the various case switches and LEDs to the motherboard. You will find these in a bank of connectors, usually at the bottom-right of the board

Hot tip

It's very easy to get these connections wrong. While the following is not guaranteed to be the same as on your system, it will give you a guide:

- The PLED connector powers the case power LED and connects to the PLED pins

- The RESET SW connector powers the reset switch and connects to the RESET pins

- The HDD LED connector powers the hard drive LED and connects to the HDLED pins

- The POWER SW connector powers the case on/off switch and connects to the PWRBTN pins

- The SPEAKER connector powers the case speaker and connects to the SPEAKER pins

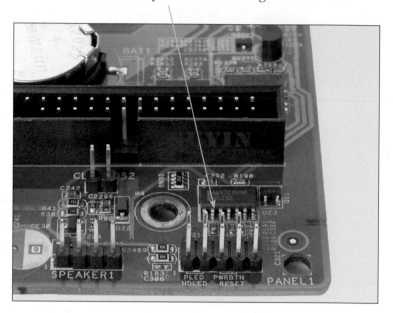

2 Switch, Speaker and LED cables shown connected to the motherboard

7 Video Systems

The video card market can be a daunting place for the uninitiated. All the hype surrounding these devices further muddies the waters. This chapter cuts through the hype, explains the difference between integrated video and sound cards, and shows you how to choose a card that will be right for your system.

Video Systems

A computer's video system is responsible for converting the stream of binary 0s and 1s from the CPU into an intelligible picture that is then passed on to the monitor.

Two types of system are used:

- Integrated video
- Video cards

Integrated Video

Integrated video is provided by the motherboard chipset. This is the type of video system commonly supplied by manufacturers of cheaper systems, as it negates the need for a separate video card that would add to the cost of the computer.

However, as video processing needs a processor and plenty of memory, and integrated video doesn't have a processor and little, or even no, memory, it has to use the system's CPU and memory. The effect of this is that the system as a whole takes a performance hit.

Also, as this type of system is primarily about cutting costs, the quality of the video produced has traditionally been on the poor side and usually only capable of producing two-dimensional displays. 3D video, such as games, has usually required the use of a dedicated video card.

However, over the last two or three years, the quality of integrated video systems has improved dramatically, to the point where they now all offer 3D capabilities. In fact, they are better than many of the video cards of not so many years ago.

That said, they still don't offer anything approaching the power and features of current video cards and, as such, are only good enough for graphics applications that are not too demanding.

For users who only want a basic system for office functions, multimedia and email, etc, integrated video will be quite adequate, and will save you the cost and bother of buying and installing a video card. You can even play 3D games as long as you accept that you will not get the best out of them in terms of frame rate, graphic effects and resolution.

Hot tip

If you are happy to settle for an integrated video system, at least go for a good one.
   At the time of writing, Intel's Extreme Graphics II, and ATI's IGP and IXP solutions, are three of the best integrated systems on the market.

Video Cards

There are two types of video card – the much touted gaming cards familiar to most people, and workstation cards. The vast majority of the ones on the market are the gaming cards.

They both provide a much higher level of video quality than integrated systems do. They also have their own processor and memory and so are not reliant on the system's CPU and memory. As a result, the system's overall performance level is better.

Gaming cards are designed with speed as one of the main criteria and provide features that are geared specifically to getting the best out of resource intensive 3D games.

Workstation video cards are intended for heavy duty stuff and provide a greater level of accuracy and performance. For example, they can supply seriously high resolutions up to a massive 3840 x 2400, which are needed by some business applications.

They are tested and certified for use with major 3D and video applications. The manufacturers also offer much better technical support. Typical applications are professional level desktop publishing, computer aided drawing (CAD) and real time video editing.

While 3D is catered for, they offer exceptional 2D performance, which is usually far more important in a business environment.

2D versus 3D

It is all too easy to be taken in by the hype surrounding video cards and lose sight of the basics. While there is no dispute regarding the importance of 3D video, it is a fact that it's only critical to hardcore gamers and a handful of other applications. For most PC uses, and hence users, good 2D video is actually the more important of the two.

So before you succumb to the slick marketing, ask yourself what it is that you spend the majority of your computing time doing. Is it playing 3D games or more mundane stuff such as basic Windows operations, office applications, email and web browsing, etc?

Beware

Video cards are the most hyped part of a computer system and, if you listen to it, you'll probably end up buying an expensive model that provides a level of performance that you are never going to need.

Don't forget

For the majority of users, good 2D performance is of far more importance than 3D. While an integrated video system will give you reasonably good 2D, a video card with a quality, high-speed RAMDAC chip, will improve 2D performance tremendously.

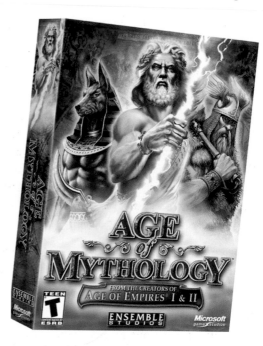

If it's the latter, then you need to be more concerned with your computer's 2D capabilities. They are the type of things that 3D has little effect on, whereas 2D does. Good 2D performance will improve image quality, text will be sharper and basic things such as window manipulation will be quicker.

While integrated video provides reasonable 2D performance it is nowhere near as good as that provided by a video card. This is why power and corporate users, who often have no need for 3D, will always have a high-quality video card in their system.

The part of the video card that is responsible for 2D is the Random Access Memory Digital to Analogue Converter (RAMDAC) chip. This is the specification that you need to look at if you want above average 2D capability – see page 82.

The Video Card Market

When you investigate the video card market, you'll quickly notice that there are a tremendous number of cards on offer, and may wonder how on earth you're going to pick one out.

However, the choice is not nearly as big as it may appear. This is because many of the cards are, to all intents and purposes, identical. The reason for this is that virtually all of them use the same basic architecture – the global processing unit (GPU), otherwise known as the chip.

For example, take the following cards:

- Asustek GeForce 7900 GTX,
- Gainward GeForce 7900 GTX
- Gigabyte Geforce 7900 GTX

Although they are three different cards from three different manufacturers, they are essentially the same because they are all driven, and controlled by, the GeForce 7900 GTX chip. The only differences between them will be in the quality of the manufacturer's control circuitry and the specifications of associated components. For example, the Asustek may offer 256 MB of memory, while the Gainward may have only 128 MB.

The vast majority of the chips used by video card manufacturers are provided by two companies: ATI (the Radeon) and Nvidia (the GeForce).

Both companies offer several versions of each chip they produce – low-end, mid-range and high-end, to cater for different sections of the market. For example, ATI offers three versions of the Radeon 9800 – the 9800 (low-end), the 9800 PRO (mid-range), and the 9800 XT (high-end).

The differences between the chip versions are determined largely by the following specifications.

- RAMDAC
- Memory capacity
- Memory type
- Memory clock speed
- Processor clock speed

We'll look at these next.

Hot tip

In most cases, the chip used is specified in the product name, e.g. the Chaintech GeForce FX 5500. Here, the manufacturer is Chaintech, the video chip is the GeForce, and the chip version is FX5500.

Video Card Specifications

We will concentrate here on gaming cards. Workstation cards are really a different entity as they are designed specifically for business applications.

Don't forget

Workstation video cards can cost $2000 and more. The level of performance they provide, and features such as massive resolutions, will never be needed by the home user.

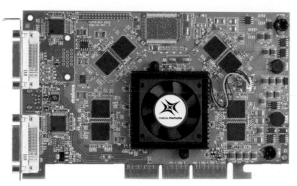

The Parhelia workstation video card from Matrox

Courtesy of Matrox Graphics Incorporated

When shopping for a video card, you need to consider the following specifications:

RAMDAC

The RAMDAC is a chip that converts the PC's digital signals into the analog signals required by CRT monitors. It also plays a major role in the quality of a card's 2D performance and the range of display refresh rates provided.

What you are looking for with regard to this device is speed – the higher the better. Anything over 300 MHz will be fine, while 400 MHz will give you superb performance.

You may notice that some video cards have two RAMDACs. This is because they can support two monitors – one RAMDAC for each.

Memory Capacity

A video card's memory capacity is often referred to as the Frame Buffer in the specifications. As a general rule, the amount of memory doesn't have a great impact on the card's speed. What it does affect is the maximum screen resolution provided by the card, and the depth of colors that the display can render.

For most applications, including the majority of 3D games, a card with 128 MB of memory will be perfectly adequate. The same card with 256 MB will not be noticeably faster.

Hot tip

Look for a video card with at least 128 MB of memory. There are still older cards on the market offering 68 MB and even 32 MB.

Type of Memory

Most cards currently on the market use DDR memory, but some are now using DDR2, and a few of the latest high-end cards are using the superfast DDR3.

The PC games currently being released are able to utilize DDR3, so this is what you will be looking for if you play any of these. Older games were not designed to take advantage of DDR3 and while they should run faster, it will not be enough to justify the high cost of the cards using this type of memory.

For most users, a card offering DDR or DDR2 memory, will be quite adequate.

Memory Clock Speed

In the same way that high-speed system memory increases the speed and performance of a computer, high-speed video memory does the same for video cards.

Low-end cards come in at around 400 to 500 MHz, mid-range cards at 800 MHz and the latest high-end cards at up to 1.8 GHz.

Processor Clock Speed

This is often referred to as the Core Clock Speed in the specifications and refers to the speed at which the Global Processing Unit (GPU) runs. As with a CPU, the faster it is, the faster the speed and the better the performance of the card.

Low-end video cards have a GPU running at about 250 MHz, mid-range cards at 450 MHz and the latest top-end cards between 600 and 700 MHz.

Vertices/Triangles

Nvidia use the term "vertices" and ATI use "triangles". Both refer to the triangular shaped objects that are used to construct a curved 3D image (the more of these there are, the more sharply defined the curve).

A top-end card uses seven to eight hundred million triangles, while a low-end card uses about 60 million.

Hot tip

Another specification that is a useful indicator of a video card's capabilities is its "Fill Rate".

This indicates the speed at which the card can render a scene and top-end ones will have a fill rate of ten billion texels per second. Low-end cards will come in at around one billion texels per second.

More Factors to Consider

Interfaces

Most video cards currently use the AGP (Advanced Graphics Port) socket on the motherboard to connect to the system. This is a high-speed data bus designed specifically to handle the huge amounts of data associated with video.

There are two things to be aware of with AGP:

1) The first is speed. AGP is available in four speeds – 1x, 2x, 4x and 8x, with 8x being the fastest. Virtually all motherboards support 8x; not all video cards do though – many low-end cards run at 4x. However, as 8x provides a data transfer rate that few current applications can fully utilize, effectively, there is little performance differential between 8x and 4x.

2) Not all motherboards provide AGP, although most do. Some of the ones offering integrated video do not provide a video card socket at all, while others provide only a PCI-Express socket (see below). So if you decide on an AGP card, check that your motherboard has an AGP socket

In the never ending quest for ever higher speeds, AGP is now being phased out in favor of the newer PCI-Express interface, which has a much faster data transfer rate than AGP 8x. Many video cards now coming on to the market use this new interface.

It has to be said though, that as most current applications (including most games) can't utilize even AGP 8x fully, they certainly don't need PCI-Express. The only users who may see any benefits from it are power-users who run applications such as CAD and video-editing, that require very high data transfer rates.

However, PCI-Express is here to stay and, as most of the motherboards equipped with this new interface also offer an AGP socket for backward compatibility, you may as well get a board that has it – a couple of years down the line you may well find that you need it.

Ports

Video cards come with a range of input and output ports, the number of which depend on the quality of the card. Budget cards will probably have only one – the VGA output to the monitor. Better cards will also have some, or all, of the following ports:

- Digital Video Interface (DVI)
- Dual-Digital Video Interface
- Video-in/Video-out (VIVO)
- Video Graphics Array (VGA)
- Dual-Video Graphics Array
- Digital Video Interface and Video Graphics Array

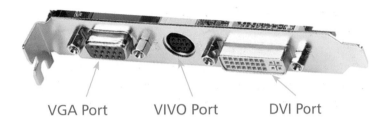

VGA Port   VIVO Port   DVI Port

Digital Video Interface (DVI)

The white DVI port is designed for use with LCD monitors, which need a digital signal. So if you are planning to use an LCD monitor, it will be handy if the video card provides one of these – see top margin note.

Video-in/Video-out (VIVO)

The VIVO (video in/video out) port enables you to hook up the PC to other video devices such as a television set, which can be useful if a larger display area is needed.

It is also possible to connect a VCR to this port to import analog video – handy for digitizing those old VHS holiday movies.

Video Graphics Array (VGA)

The blue VGA port is used by CRT monitors and will be found on the vast majority of video cards. If the motherboard provides integrated video, there will be a VGA port on its output panel.

Some cards also have dual-VGA or dual-DVI ports (or one of each). This is known as dual-video and allows you to run two monitors from the same card. This can be useful in many situations; a writer, for example, can have his word processor open on one screen and his reference material open on the other.

So before you buy your card, consider whether any of the above ports or combinations, may be of use to you, and if so, make sure the card supplies it.

Beware

It is not essential to have a DVI equipped video card in order to use an LCD monitor. All LCD monitors will accept an analog signal (via the blue VGA port) from the video card, but will need to convert it to digital form themselves. This procedure will result in a very slight reduction in picture quality.

Don't forget

If you have a spare monitor, consider getting a video card with dual outputs. This will enable you to run both monitors at the same time, which can be very useful in certain situations.

Dimensions

Many of the top-end video cards are serious pieces of circuitry and by this we don't just mean specifications, we mean big, as in take up a lot of room. This is further compounded by the also serious cooling systems these cards require.

Beware

If you go for one of the latest video cards, make sure it will leave room for the other devices you intend to install. Some of these cards come with quite monstrous cooling systems that will occupy an inordinate amount of space in the case.

A video card with two massive heatsinks, one on each side, plus a fan, making it an extremely bulky device

When fitted into the video socket, these cards can completely block access to the nearest PCI socket, which means your motherboard will effectively have one less. There are also a few cards that not only use the video socket, but also the adjacent PCI socket. Again, you are one PCI socket short.

If you intend to buy one of the top-end cards, don't forget to check the dimensions of the card when planning what other expansion cards you are going to install. If you don't, you might just find yourself a socket short.

Application Programming Interfaces (APIs)

APIs are basically a set of routines that programmers use to ensure that their software is supported by as wide a range of hardware setups as possible. In relation to video, they allow multimedia applications to utilize hardware acceleration features provided by video systems.

For the API, and thus the application, to work, it must be supported by the PC's video system.

There are various APIs, such as OpenGL and Microsoft's DirectX. The latter is the one most commonly used, so you should ensure that your video card supports the latest version of it.

For the gamers amongst you, games using OpenGL are reckoned to run slightly better on Nvidia video cards, whereas DirectX games are better with ATI cards.

Power and Heat Issues

Power and heat are only issues if you are buying at the top end of the video card market.

The more features packed into a video card, the more power required to run it. You need to consider this when purchasing the power supply unit. You may, for example, find that you need a 450 watt PSU instead of a 400 watt version – the extra 50 watts to cover the power requirement of the card.

Furthermore, all this power generates lots of heat. While the card's cooling system will keep it cool, this heat will raise the temperature in the system case, and because of this, you may need to install extra fans or invest in a more efficient cooling system.

Bundled Extras

Many video cards come with useful "extras" that can help to soften the impact on your wallet.

TV tuners are popular PC add-ons and allow you to watch television in a resizable window. While these can be purchased as a separate device, buying a video card with one built-in is a cheaper option. This has the added benefit of freeing up a PCI slot that would otherwise be needed for the TV tuner card, not to mention the bother of installing it.

A good example is the Radeon All-in-Wonder series from ATI.

Extra software can include media applications that enable you to view TV (from a tuner card), DVDs, pictures, and video clips. Also included with some cards is an infrared remote control.

Hot tip

Microsoft release updated versions of DirectX periodically. You can find out what the latest version is (and download it) by going to www.microsoft.com/directx.

Hot tip

Most video cards include a couple of games in the box. While they are never the latest, some of them are fairly recent. If you are torn between two cards, the games on offer might be a deciding factor.

Installing a Video Card

The procedure is the same whether you are installing an AGP card or a PCI-Express card. Here, we are using an AGP model.

 Remove the board from the antistatic bag, holding it at the edges – see top margin note

 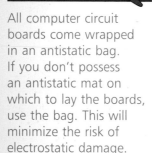

 Locate the colored AGP (or PCI-Express) socket

3 Open the retaining clip – see margin note

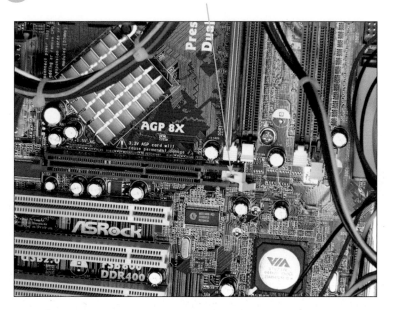

Hot tip

High-end video cards are heavy and bulky devices due to the large cooling systems that they use. To prevent them pulling out of the socket, many motherboards these days supply a retaining clip.

4 Slide the board into the socket. When it is fully inserted the retaining clip will close automatically

...cont'd

5 Screw the backplate to the case chassis

Having installed the video card, you now need to connect the monitor to it – see page 98. It will also need setting up in the BIOS – see page 165.

When you run the system for the first time, you will need to install the card's driver and configure it to suit your applications.

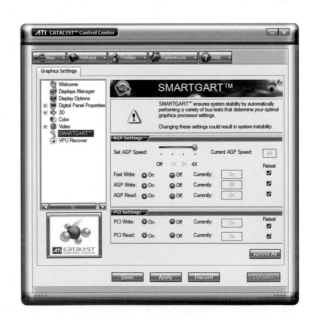

8 Monitors

When it comes to buying a monitor, you basically have two choices – Cathode-Ray Tube (CRT) or Liquid Crystal Display (LCD). Each has its pros and cons.

Overview

Considering it gets more attention than any other part of a computer system, it is surprising just how many people pay scant regard to the monitor when purchasing their PC. Usually, the CPU and the video system are of much more interest to them.

Don't forget

It is a fact that most PC applications do not require a high-resolution monitor. Those of you building a low-end system, or working to a budget, can make economies here. Cash saved can be put towards something that is more important – extra memory, for example.

Image reprinted with permission from ViewSonic Corporation

This fact is well known to manufacturers and they take advantage by tending to supply rather cheap monitors with their pre-built systems, as they do with keyboards and mice. Typically, these monitors will provide limited resolutions and refresh rates, inferior picture quality and poor power regulation.

Hot tip

If you are looking to make savings wherever possible, you can buy monitors that come with integrated speakers. They won't be of very good quality, but will, nevertheless, be perfectly adequate for Window's jingles, etc.
   Another handy feature to look out for is a built-in USB hub that will increase your connection options.

However, it must be said that for most applications they are perfectly adequate and for the self-builder looking to save money where possible, these low-end monitors do provide an opportunity to do this, as long as he or she is prepared to put up with their limitations.

When the first edition of this book was written, CRT monitors were the most prevalent type, due mainly to the cost and limitations of their LCD counterparts. Today, however, the situation is completely different and LCDs have all but taken over the monitor market.

However, there is still life in the CRT and this is because they have some characteristics that make them the more suitable type for certain applications. Furthermore, all is not sweetness and light with LCDs, as they do have some serious drawbacks.

CRT or LCD?

Choosing between the two is the first decision to make, and to ensure you get it right, the following factors must be considered.

Supported Resolutions

A monitor's resolution is the number of pixels that comprise the image, and is expressed in terms of width x height. Commonly used resolutions are 1024 x 768, 1280 x 1024 and 1600 x 1200.

CRT monitors are able to support all of these, plus many others, all at a high level of image quality. LCDs however, can support only one resolution at high quality. This is known as the native, or fixed, resolution. The native resolutions for the various sizes of LCD monitors are as follows:

- 15-inch monitors – native resolution 1024 x 768
- 17- and 19-inch monitors – native resolution 1280 x 1024
- 20- and 21-inch monitors – native resolution 1600 x 1200
- 23-inch monitors – native resolution 1920 x 1200

Due to this limitation, the size of the LCD you buy will be determined largely by its native resolution – it must be one that you are comfortable with and that is suitable for your applications.

Note that while LCDs can support a small number of other resolutions, they are achieved by interpolation techniques (similar to those used by scanner manufacturers) that result in a much lower quality display.

Don't forget

The issue of screen resolution is one of the biggest drawbacks of LCD monitors, as they only provide a good picture at one resolution.

What this all boils down to is that if you run applications that require different resolutions, a CRT has to be the choice. For example, gamers find that certain games play better at one resolution than they do at others.

However, if the native resolution provided by a particular LCD is acceptable for all your applications, this won't be an issue and your choice will be determined by other factors.

...cont'd

Beware

If you are a gamer, or watch video on the PC, you need to be aware of a serious limitation with LCD monitors; namely, their slow pixel response rate. This can have a serious impact on the quality of video playback. Look for a figure of 16 ms or less.

Response Rate

The next thing to consider is the monitor's response rate. This is a measure of how long it takes the device to respond to changes in the display. If it responds too slowly, the result is a blurred image.

As can be imagined, this is a very important factor when playing games or watching video.

Because CRTs have an instantaneous response rate, this issue is not a problem with these monitors. With LCDs, however, which react more slowly, it most certainly is.

So if you want an LCD, and intend to play games or watch video, you must get one with a fast response rate. The generally accepted limit is 16 ms; if it is any higher than this, you will experience picture degradation.

Be aware that many current LCD monitors have a response time well above 16 ms, so this is something that you must check out in the specifications. Furthermore, do not assume that because a particular LCD is expensive, it will have a low response rate.

Image Quality

Here, honors are about even. LCDs produce an image of startling clarity and crispness that CRTs cannot match (although it is a fact that many people prefer the softer look of a CRT display).

In terms of color reproduction, CRTs can display a wider range of colors than LCDs. This makes them more suitable for those who work with graphics or, indeed, any application in which accurate color reproduction is important. Note that we are talking about low-end LCDs here – high-end models can be as good as CRTs.

Dimensions

One of the biggest advantages of LCDs is their depth, typically, two to three inches in comparison to some 16 inches for a 17-inch CRT. This allows them to be pushed much further back, thus creating more usable desk space. It also makes them much lighter, and thus easier to transport.

Don't forget

Lack of desktop "real estate" is one good reason to go for an LCD monitor.

Brightness

LCDs have a higher level of inherent brightness that makes them much easier to view in natural lighting conditions. Most also come with a special screen coating that reduces glare.

So if it's a nice sunny day, you don't have to draw the curtains to keep the sunlight off the screen.

Viewing Angle

CRTs can be viewed from any angle and while the sharper the angle, the less you can see, the image itself doesn't deteriorate.

This is not the case with LCDs. With these, there is a noticeable loss of image quality when the monitor is viewed from an angle. It is not a major issue but it is, nevertheless, there.

Good quality LCDs have a viewing angle of 160 to 180 degrees. Low-end models have viewing angles as low as 60 degrees.

Power Requirements

LCD monitors are much more efficient in terms of energy consumption. The power requirement for these devices is about a third of that of CRTs. A welcome side-effect of this is that they produce less heat.

Radiation

CRT monitors do emit a certain amount of low-frequency radiation. Some people think this can be harmful, others don't. If you use an LCD monitor, the issue becomes irrelevant as these devices emit virtually no radiation.

Cost

While LCDs have come down in price dramatically in recent years, they are still slightly more expensive than a CRT offering a similar level of performance and features.

Don't forget

If two or more people tend to view the monitor at the same time, the viewing angle limitation of LCDs should be taken into account.

Hot tip

CRT monitors come in two types – Shadow Mask and Aperture Grille. Aperture Grille monitors are more expensive, but provide a better picture due to superior beam filtering technology.

Image Quality

The factors considered so far should have made up your mind regarding which type of monitor to go for. However, none of them relate to the most important factor of all – image quality.

Consideration of the following specifications will ensure that your new monitor delivers a high-quality picture.

Dot Pitch

This is a measure of the distance between the individual pixels that comprise the display and is the best indicator of a monitor's image quality. The lower the figure, the greater the sharpness and color clarity of the displayed image.

High-quality CRTs will have a dot pitch around 0.21 mm, while low-end models will be around 0.28 mm. A value of 0.26 mm provides a reasonable picture; monitors with a higher dot pitch than this should be left on the shelf.

With LCDs, look for a figure no higher than 0.29 mm; 0.26 mm will give a top-quality display.

Contrast Ratio (LCDs Only)

This is the measurement of the difference in light intensity between the brightest (white) and darkest (black) tones, it provides a good indication of an LCD's image quality.

A high contrast ratio will result in an image that is vibrant and colorful. If it is too low, the image will look faded and washed-out. The lowest figure you should accept is 350:1. High-quality LCDs will have a ratio of 600:1 and above.

Dead Pixels (LCDs Only)

A final consideration with LCDs is the issue of dead pixels. Pixels are the tiny elements that form the display of a monitor. If one is damaged and thus doesn't work, it stands out from the ones that surround it as a dot of a different color. This was a considerable problem with early LCDs and buyers were expected to accept a number of dead pixels.

These days, it is less of an issue as LCD technology has improved. However, it is still common to get an LCD with one or two dead pixels and so it is worth finding out what a manufacturer's policy is regarding this before parting with the cash. Many will replace the monitor, but some won't.

Don't forget

For a top-quality CRT display, look for a dot pitch rating of 0.21 mm or 0.22 mm.
   With LCDs, the figure should be 0.26 mm.

Hot tip

Before you buy an LCD monitor, we suggest that you check out the manufacturer's policy regarding dead pixels. Some people can live with them, others can't.

WideScreen LCD Monitors

The introduction of Microsoft's Windows Media Center Edition, has made it much more intuitive for users to use their PC to watch TV, listen to radio, digitally record TV programs, watch commercial DVDs, convert analog video to digital video, organize and play music, etc.

Products like this are rapidly turning the PC into a fully-fledged home entertainment center, and widescreen LCD monitors have taken the process further.

Beware

If you are a gamer looking to capitalize on the advantages offered by widescreen monitors, be aware that the game manufacturers are only just catching on. It will be a while yet before PC games are commonly available in the wide-screen format.

Most models are capable of playing high definition TV, and some even come with a built-in TV tuner for which a remote control is usually supplied.

Picture-in-picture and picture-by-picture displays are common in this class of monitor. SRS WOW sound is another feature often available and provides sound quality that is much superior to that usually delivered by built-in monitor speakers.

Widescreen monitors add another dimension to game playing in the same way they do with any other type of video. While, currently, there are few games that will play in this format, this is set to change as these devices become more mainstream.

With regard to PC functions, the main advantage they offer is a much increased viewing area, which enables two applications to be open side by side, each in a large, easily viewable, window.

Hot tip

A widescreen monitor will be a real boon for users who need to have two applications open at the same time.

Installing a Monitor

CRT Monitors

These use the blue VGA connection and connect to either the video card or to the motherboard's integrated video system.

Video card connection

Integrated video connection

LCD Monitors

These can use both VGA and DVI connections. If your system has a DVI equipped video card, this is the one to use as shown below. Otherwise, use the VGA connection as shown above.

Beware

If your PC has both a video card and integrated video, make sure that you connect the monitor to the correct one. This is a very common mistake and is easily done.

DVI output from the video card

9 Testing the Basic System

The guts of your new PC are now in place. Hopefully, you haven't made any mistakes so far. If you have, they must be rectified before you proceed further. Here, we show you the likely problems and how to resolve them.

Hot tip

If your motherboard has an integrated video system, you can use this and leave the video card out for the time being. This will be one less potential cause of problems at this stage.

Once the basic system is operational, you can then install the video card and run the test again. If it fails, you'll know immediately that the video card is the source of the problem.

Beware

Without a keyboard connected to the system, the computer will not boot-up.

Beware

Don't be tempted to install everything in one go and hope it all works.

Unless you've built computers before, this is not the way to do it.

Why Do This Now?

At the moment, your system consists of the power supply unit, motherboard, CPU, memory and video card (as shown below). This is the minimum required to get a display on the monitor. However, before you go any further you also need to connect the keyboard to the system (without it the PC will refuse to boot).

Having connected the keyboard, if you now test the system and it fails to work you know the problem lies with one of the above devices.

You can, of course, take the optimistic approach and build the system completely by installing all the other parts, such as the hard drive, removable disk drives, and peripherals as well. If it works, fine. However, if it does not, you will then be faced with many more potential causes for the failure. For example, a hard drive that hasn't been configured correctly can prevent the computer from booting.

To keep head scratching to the minimum, you should test each device as you install it (where possible) and make sure it works before moving on to the next. There is nothing wrong with optimism, but a more pragmatic approach may well save you time in the end.

Check the Monitor

It really would be a complete waste of time to troubleshoot a system that seemingly refuses to boot-up, when all along the problem is a malfunctioning or incorrectly adjusted monitor.

Therefore, this is the stage at which you check this device. To help you do it, all modern monitors will display a message or splash screen of some sort when switched on to indicate they are operational. For this to work, however, the monitor must be isolated from the computer, i.e. the signal cable must be disconnected from the video system's output socket.

Check it out as follows:

 1 Plug the monitor's power cable into the wall socket. Switch it on, give it a few seconds to warm up and then you should see a test signal similar to the one below

Don't forget

Before the monitor will display a test screen, it must be isolated from the computer.

> No signal input
> or
> Cable disconnected

Hot tip

If you are in any doubt about a monitor, another way to test it is by connecting it to a different system.

101

Hot tip

If you cannot get anything on the monitor, check that the contrast and brightness controls haven't been turned right down inadvertently.

If you don't see a test signal and the monitor lights are off, then either the monitor itself is faulty or it is not getting any power. Check the power supply, plug, and cable. If these are all OK then the monitor must be faulty.

If you do see a light on the monitor, make sure it's not simply in Standby mode. Press the power switch again.

When you do have a working monitor, hook it up to the system as shown on page 98.

Beware

Monitors carry high voltages that can be lethal. These voltages will remain until discharged. Never open up a monitor for any reason.

Check the Connections

Before you switch your system on for the first time, it may be as well to check all the connections. It is not encouraging to be greeted by a blank screen at the first attempt.

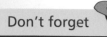 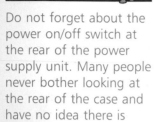

Do not forget about the power on/off switch at the rear of the power supply unit. Many people never bother looking at the rear of the case and have no idea there is even one there.

A blank screen is not what you want to see when you first switch on

Hot tip

One of the most likely things to get wrong is the computer's on/off switch connection to the motherboard. This will be in a row of 2-pin connectors (see page 76) and it is very easy to pick the wrong one.

So, check the following:

- The PC is plugged into a wall socket
- The switch at the rear of the power supply unit is on
- The monitor is plugged into a wall socket
- The monitor's signal cable is connected to the video system
- The PC's on/off switch is connected to the correct terminals on the motherboard
- The motherboard is connected to the power supply unit
- The RAM modules are seated in their sockets and held in place by the retaining clips
- The CPU fan is connected to the motherboard

If everything appears to be OK, the moment of truth has arrived. It's time to switch on and see what happens.

Does it Work?

Go on then, hit the switch. What you see next depends on the BIOS chip in your system – see margin note. If your system has an AWARD BIOS, you should see the following on the screen:

```
Phoenix — AwardBIOS v6.00PC, An Energy Star Ally
Copyright © 1984–2003, Phoenix Technologies, Ltd

KM266M.B12 For KM266-MNB

Main Processor : AMD Athlon 1200Mhz
Memory Testing : 262144K OK

    Primary Master : None
     Primary Slave : None
  Secondary Master : None
   Secondary Slave : None



Press Del to enter SETUP
10/09/2003-KM266-8235-6A6LVP8CC-00
```

If you have an AMI BIOS, you should see this or similar:

```
VIA Technologies, Inc. VIA VT8237 Serial ATA RAID BIOS Setting
Copyright © VIA Technologies, Inc. All Rights Reserved

Scan Devices. Please Wait ...
Press < Tab > Key into User Window
Serial_Ch0 Master:
Serial_Ch0 Master:
```

Both displays indicate that you're off to a good start. The fact that you can see text on the screen shows that all the components are functioning correctly.

Hot tip

In this chapter you will see several references to the BIOS. This is a chip on the motherboard that carries out a series of routines that starts the computer. These include identifying all the hardware in the system, and checking that they are working correctly.

Hot tip

If you have an AWARD BIOS in your system, as the computer boots-up you should hear a long single beep. This is one of a series of beep codes (see page 106), and indicates that the BIOS has found no problems.

This is not the case with AMI BIOSs, though – a beep indicates a fault.

...cont'd

Beware

One problem that you may encounter is the boot procedure stopping with a floppy drive error message. This will be because you haven't fitted one yet and some BIOSs are configured to stop if they don't find one. To override this and continue booting, press the F1 key (or the key specified on the boot screen).

The system will continue to boot and then stop with an error message. With an AWARD BIOS you will see this:

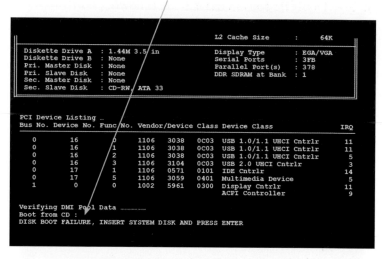

With an AMI BIOS you will see this:

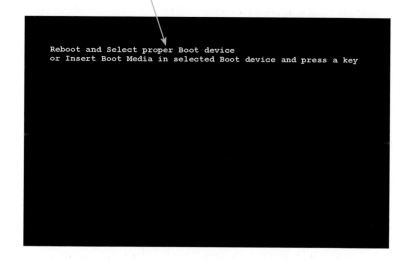

Both messages indicate a boot disk error and in this case, it is because the boot disk (hard drive) has not yet been installed.

If the system gets as far as this, then it is working as it should and you can give yourself a pat on the back. The next stage will be installing the hard drive (see pages 117-123) and then setting it up and installing the operating system (see pages 160-162). If, however, it does not, then go on to the next page.

Hot tip

Boot screens load so quickly that it can be difficult to get any information from them. However, you can stop them by pressing the Pause key on the keyboard. To resume, press Enter.

The PC Doesn't Boot-Up

Things have not gone as planned. The PC either doesn't boot at all or doesn't reach the boot disk error message stage as shown on page 104. Troubleshoot as follows:

The System is Dead

First, make sure it really is "dead". Check that none of the LEDs on the case or keyboard are lit, the PSU/CPU fans are not running, and that the PC is not making any beeping sounds.

If there are absolutely no signs of life, then you have a power supply fault. Check the following:

- Is there power at the wall socket? Plug another appliance into it. If that works, the PC is getting power

- Check the fuse in the power cable plug

- Is the power cable OK? Try replacing it (many house-hold appliances use the same type)

- Check that the PSU on/off switch at the top-rear of the system case is not in the off position

If these all check out then, sadly, the power supply unit is defective and will need replacing.

The System is Alive but the Screen is Blank

The system is powered up but there is nothing on the screen – this is the more likely scenario.

A faulty or incorrectly installed motherboard, CPU, memory module or video card can all be the cause of a blank display. Fortunately, when the BIOS finds a major part that is not working, it advises the user accordingly in the form of a series of coded beeps, known not surprisingly as beep codes.

NOTE: a single beep is normal with AWARD BIOSs and indicates that the BIOS has found no problems. You will hear this every time at start-up. This is not the case with AMI BIOSs though – one beep with these indicates a memory problem.

The BIOS chip manufacturers all have their own versions of these codes so you will first need to establish the manufacturer of your BIOS chip. This information will be found in the motherboard manual. It might also be stamped on the chip itself.

Hot tip

Absolutely the first thing to check when your PC appears to be dead is the power supply. Don't forget to check the external AC supply as well.

Hot tip

The easiest way to establish that your power supply unit is operational is to check that the fan is working and that the system case lights are on.

Beep Codes

Having done so, find the code you are hearing in the table below. This will isolate the faulty component.

Hot tip

The BIOS chip has a built-in diagnostic utility that alerts you to any problems it encounters during boot-up. It does this in two ways – a series of coded beeps if the problem occurs before the video system has initialized, or a text error message (see inside front cover) if the fault comes after.

Beeps	Fault
AWARD BIOS	
1 long, 2 short	Video system
Continuous	Memory
1 long, 3 short	Video system
AMI BIOS	
1	Memory
2	Memory
3	Memory
4	Motherboard
5	CPU
6	Motherboard
7	CPU
8	Video system
9 to 11	Motherboard

Troubleshooting Motherboards

If the beep codes indicate a problem with the motherboard, the first thing to check is that the CPU's fan is running. This will confirm that the board is receiving power from the power supply unit. If it isn't, check that the fan is connected to its power socket (see bottom margin note on page 30) and that the power cable from the PSU is connected to the motherboard (see page 75).

Next, try reseating the CPU in its socket. Do the same with the memory modules even if the beep code is not specific to either.

Check that you haven't dropped something metallic, such as a screw or washer, into the board when installing it. This could create a short-circuit that may prevent it from working.

Do the keyboard LEDs come on? If they don't, the board is almost certainly faulty. If they do, this indicates that the board is active, in which case the problem is more likely to be with the CPU or memory.

Hot tip

Before condemning a motherboard, it is always worth checking that the CPU and memory modules are firmly seated in their respective sockets.

There is also the possibility of not hearing any beeps at all. This means nothing with an AMI BIOS but with an AWARD BIOS it is significant.

In the latter case, make sure the case speaker is connected to the correct motherboard terminals. If there are still no beeps, then you definitely have a problem with the motherboard. This will be confirmed if the keyboard and case LEDs are dead as well.

Troubleshooting the Video System

If you are using an integrated video system then you have no option but to replace the motherboard as it is part of the board.

If you are using a video card, the first thing to check is that the monitor cable is securely connected to the card's output socket. If the PC also has integrated video, make sure you haven't connected the monitor to this by mistake.

Reseat the card and make sure it is pushed home completely.

If you still have no luck, there is one more option open to you, assuming your motherboard has an integrated video system. Switch the computer off and remove the video card from the system. Then connect the monitor cable to the integrated system's output. Switch on, and if you now have video then the video card is faulty.

Troubleshooting Memory

If the beep code indicates a memory problem, the first thing to do is make sure the module is fitted correctly (as described on pages 40-42).

Next, install the module into a different slot and try again. It isn't unheard of for a memory socket to be faulty.

If the problem persists then the module is damaged and will need replacing. If you have installed two modules, try removing one of them and restarting. If the PC still doesn't work, replace it with the other one. While it is unlikely, if one of the modules is damaged, it could prevent the other one from working.

Otherwise, replace the module with a new one as you have almost certainly damaged it by careless handling.

Don't forget

No beeps at all with an AWARD BIOS, assuming the PC has power and the case speaker is correctly connected, is a certain indicator of a motherboard failure.

Don't forget

If you are experiencing video card problems, try removing the card and connecting the video cable to the motherboard's integrated video system (if there is one). If you now get text on the screen, then the video card is faulty and will need replacing.

Boot-up Doesn't Complete

By this we mean the boot procedure starts but doesn't reach the boot disk error message stage, which is as far as it can go without a hard drive and operating system.

However, you will at least be seeing text on the screen, which indicates the motherboard, CPU, and video system are all operational. This leaves only the memory as a potential cause of the problem and, in all likelihood, boot-up will stop at the memory test stage, as shown below.

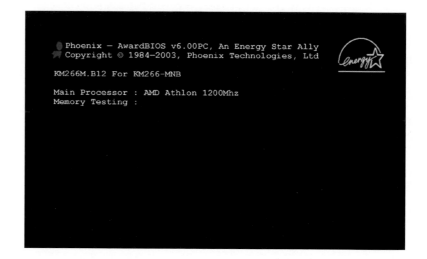

Troubleshoot as described on page 107.

As a general note, assuming the components you are installing are all new, the likelihood of any of them being faulty is very remote. It is far more likely that any problems will be connection issues.

The most common mistakes here are incorrect fitting of the case switches to the motherboard, connecting the monitor to the wrong video system (integrated instead of the video card, or vice versa) and damaging the memory module/s by careless handling.

As a final note, be aware that troubleshooting PC hardware is restricted to identifying and then replacing the faulty board or component. Repairing them is not an option.

10 Hard Drives

In this chapter, you'll learn about the various interfaces used by these devices and important specifications – factors that need to be considered when buying a drive. We also look at partitioning and formatting, and drive configuration, including RAID setups.

Overview

The hard drive is where all your data is stored, so if it fails – and when they do, it is almost always terminal – all that data is lost.

Bear in mind, also, that these are mechanical devices, so the one thing you can be certain about is that they will fail eventually.

These two facts make it absolutely critical that you get the best quality hard drive you can afford. This is not a component to cut costs on. Don't even think about budget or second-hand models.

Hot tip

You are well advised to spend your money on a low-capacity drive of high quality, rather than a low-quality drive that has a huge capacity, which in all likelihood you will never use anyway.

When buying a hard drive you need to consider the following:

- Interface – USB, FireWire, ATA, SATA or SCSI
- Type – external or internal
- Specifications
- Storage capacity
- Configurations

Interfaces

Advanced Technology Attachment (ATA)

The standard drive interface for many years now, ATA originated back in 1986 and has since undergone many evolutions, which have increased the speed and size of the drives that it can support.

This interface can be a perplexing topic as it has several different names and versions, all of which essentially indicate the same thing. Much confusion is caused by the fact that it is often referred to as EIDE (Enhanced Integrated Drive Electronics). This is a misnomer, though, as EIDE actually refers to a device that has an integrated controller, rather than on the motherboard as used to be the norm. When you see a drive described as EIDE or IDE, it means the device uses the ATA interface.

You will also see ATA hard drives advertised as DMA and UDMA. These abbreviations stand for Direct Mode Access and Ultra Direct Mode Access, respectively. These are improved versions of the ATA interface that allow data transfer to and from the hard drive to take place with minimal input from the CPU.

The ATA interface also has different speeds, i.e. data transfer rates, with the latest (ATA-7) supporting data transfer speeds of up to 133 MB/s.

Serial ATA (SATA)

SATA is a relatively new development of the ATA interface and provides several major improvements. These include:

- Data transfer speed – the first generation of SATA, SATA I, had a data transfer speed of 150 MB/s, compared with a maximum of 133 MB/s for ATA. The current SATA generation, SATA II, transfers data at 300 MB/s, and future generations are expected to offer at least 600 MB/s

- Hot-swapping capabilities – SATA drives can be connected and disconnected while the PC is running, unlike ATA drives, which require the PC to be powered off before this can be done

- Power requirements – SATA drives have a lower power requirement than ATA drives, which in turn means that they generate less heat

...cont'd

- Setting up – SATA drives do not need to be configured in a master/slave relationship as do ATA drives (see page 117). However, they do need to be partitioned and formatted

- Improved airflow – SATA drives use a slimline interface cable that offers much less resistance to airflow than the 80-wire ribbon cables used by ATA drives

| SATA cable | ATA ribbon cable |

Small Computer System Interface (SCSI)

SCSI is completely different to ATA/SATA. It is actually a system interface as it is not limited just to disk drives – it can also be used for printers, scanners, etc.

Hard drives that use this interface are high-performance units designed to provide fast data transfer (up to 320 MB/s) and high levels of reliability. These qualities make them ideal for use in server and corporate environments, which is in fact, where they are normally seen. They are not really intended for use in home

PCs, which is why mainstream motherboards do not support SCSI.

Boards that do are designed to run high-performance CPUs, such as the Opteron and Xeon. Therefore, this type of setup is too expensive for most home users.

However, if you need the advantages offered by a SCSI hard drive, it is still possible to have one. To do it, you will need to install a SCSI host adapter PCI card (shown above) in the motherboard. Not only will this run your SCSI hard drive, you can also run other SCSI devices from it.

Beware

SCSI hard drives have a high rotational speed (typically, 15000 rpm). Side effects of this are higher noise and heat emission levels. Also, maximum storage capacities are less than with ATA and SATA drives.

Don't forget

If you wish to take advantage of the high performance levels and reliability offered by SCSI hard drives, you will need to add the SCSI interface to your system.

While the next generation of SATA hard drives will close the gap in speed, they will still be a mile away from SCSI in terms of reliability.

Although PC manufacturers are now fitting SATA hard drives in their desktop PCs, SCSI hard drives are, and will remain, the choice for servers, corporate and power-users, despite the fact that they cost four times as much as their ATA/SATA equivalents.

FireWire

FireWire (also known as IEEE 1394), is a high-speed system interface that offers data transfer rates of up to 800 MB/s. Other advantages are the ability to run up to 63 devices, no need for CPU intervention, plug-and-play support, hot-swapping support, a slim 6-wire cable and the supply of up to 45 watts of power per port allowing most devices to operate without a separate power supply.

Note that FireWire hard drives are external devices and have to be connected to a FireWire port. If the motherboard does not support FireWire, and few do, then a FireWire PCI adapter card will need to be installed. This will supply up to four ports.

Currently, FireWire is the fastest interface and it is particularly suited to high-speed multimedia applications, such as realtime audio- and video-editing, where fast data transmission is required.

Universal Serial Bus (USB)

USB is a system interface that is very similar in concept to FireWire. It will allow up to 127 devices to run simultaneously on a computer and has many of the features offered by FireWire, such as hot-swapping, plug-and-play and power provision.

As we saw on page 53, USB comes in two versions – USB 1, which has a maximum data transfer speed of 12 MB/s, and the much faster USB 2, which has a transfer rate of 480 MB/s.

USB 2 is currently the USB standard and will be found on virtually all motherboards built from 2004 onwards. While not as fast as FireWire, it is considerably faster than the ATA and SATA I interfaces.

With regard to hard drives, as with FireWire, this interface is only used by external models.

Don't forget

FireWire drives are ideal for applications that require seriously high data transmission speeds.

Hot tip

USB 2 is some forty times faster than USB 1. So if you decide on a USB hard drive, get one that supports USB 2.

Internal or External?

Internal Hard Drives

For most users, an internal hard drive will be the most practical option, for two reasons: a) they are hidden away – fit it and forget it and b) they are much cheaper than external drives.

They are available in the ATA, SATA and SCSI interfaces.

External Hard Drives

External drives need desk space of their own, cost considerably more than their internal equivalents as they need a sturdy case and often a separate power supply.

Another drawback is that while it is possible to install and run Microsoft Windows on an external hard drive, it is not an easy thing to set up. In practical terms therefore, they are restricted to additional storage purposes.

They do, however, have several advantages. First, they have much faster data transfer rates as they use either the USB or FireWire interfaces. For those who need to store and access large amounts of data, they are indispensable.

Second, data is easily transferable; unplug the drive from one PC and plug it into another. This is much simpler and quicker than transferring it via removable media.

As they are situated outside the system case, the heat they generate does not affect the PC's internal temperature.

Internal drives are limited in terms of physical size by the constraints of the system case, which in turn limits their maximum storage capacity (currently around 750 GB). External models have no such limits and so are available with capacities up to 1600 GB.

Hot tip

Note that installing the Linux and Apple Mac OS X operating systems on an external drive is a straightforward procedure.

Hot tip

External hard drives come pre-partitioned and formatted. Simply plug them in and they're ready to go.

Hot tip

External drives are available in "tough case" models that are built to withstand being dropped and otherwise physically abused.

Specifications

You should by now have decided what interface you want your new drive to use. In all probability, it will be SATA, which is what we recommend. There's nothing wrong with ATA but as SATA drives offer several worthwhile advantages, and are similarly priced, it would be pointless not to.

Having made your decision, the next move is to make sure that your chosen drive is up to the job. To do this, you need to consider the following specifications:

	Low-End	Mid-Range	Top-End
	ATA	SATA	SCSI
	100 - 133	150 - 300	320
Interface Speed (external data rate)	The speed at which data is transferred between the drive and the system. The differences between the various versions of ATA are negligible but there is a big difference between ATA/SATA I and SATA II/SCSI. Measured in MB/s		
	400 - 600	600 - 750	800 - 900
Internal Data Rate	This is the speed at which a drive's internal read channel can transfer data from the magnetic media. Internal Data Rates are measured in MB/s. More important than the interface speed		
	5400	7200	10000 - 15000
Rotational Speed	The speed at which a drive's platters spin directly affects the speed at which the drive reads and writes data. This is a critical performance factor and the faster it is the better. Measured in rpm		
	12	8.5	3.6
Access or Seek Time	The time needed to locate data on a drive's disk platters. This is an important indicator of a drive's performance. Measured in ms		
	2	2	8
Buffer or Cache Memory	The buffer is a memory cache used to store frequently accessed data to improve performance and is specified in MBs. Not critical but the larger it is, the better		

Hot tip

So you don't get confused, be aware that SATA I is often described as SATA-150, and SATA II as SATA-300.

Hot tip

It is possible to run both ATA and SATA drives in the same system as long as the motherboard supports both interfaces.

This can be handy if you want to install your operating system on a new SATA drive and use an old ATA drive for extra storage purposes.

Hot tip

Some manufacturers specify a drive's Seek Time and others specify Access Time.

Technically, there are slight differences but to all intents and purposes they can be considered to be the same.

Storage Capacity

Working out how much capacity you need is not easy, so try to be a bit scientific about it. As every GB costs money, you don't want to buy more than you are ever likely to use. Take a look at your present system, see how many GBs you have used, and then add on whatever you think you are likely to need in the future.

When doing this, bear in mind that each successive version of virtually all major software titles are larger than the ones that preceded them. Remember, also, that video and graphics eat up hard drive space at an alarming rate.

When you've arrived at a figure, add 30 per cent to it. The reason for doing this is that hard drives only perform efficiently at up to about 70 per cent of their capacity. Any higher than this and data transfer rates start slowing down.

Aesthetics

This is only relevant to external drives. As with other visible parts of the system, these devices are now available in some eye-catching designs. Whereas once you would probably have shoved the ugly box behind something to hide it, now you might actually give it a prominent position on your desk. Some interesting examples are shown below.

Hot tip

Modern hard drives provide a tremendous amount of storage capacity – external models up to 1600 GB and internal models up to 750 GB.

However, with the exception of Windows XP (1.5 GB) and Windows Vista (8 GB), virtually no software uses more than 1 GB of disk space.

For typical home-users, therefore, 40-60 GB will be ample. The only time anyone is likely to need higher capacity is when the PC is used to store large amounts of high-resolution video or images.

Don't forget

If you use 70 per cent or more of a hard drive's capacity, its performance will start dropping off. Bear this in mind when making your decision regarding the capacity you are likely to need.

ATA Drive Configuration

ATA hard drives have to be configured before they can be used. In a single-drive setup, the drive will be the master, in a two-drive setup, one will be the master and the other the slave.

To facilitate this, ATA drives have a jumper block at the rear with four pairs of pins, each pair providing a different configuration that is selected by means of a 2-pin jumper.

Hot tip

SATA hard drives do not need to be configured in a master/slave relationship.

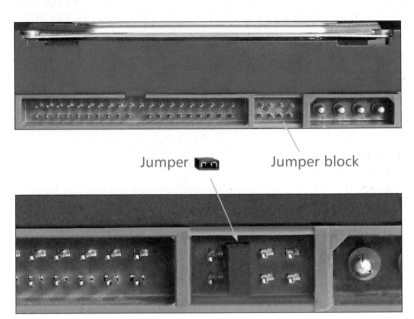

Jumper   Jumper block

Most drives are supplied with the jumper already set to the master position so, if you intend to install just one drive, all you need to do is check that the jumper is in this position. Do it by referring to the jumper/pin table (shown right), which you will find on the drive case.

However, if you are going to install two drives, then you must choose the one you want as the master (the better or newer of the two) and place the jumpers on both accordingly. Also, the master drive should be the one on which the operating system is to be installed.

Don't forget

The hard drive must be correctly jumpered for the intended purpose, i.e. master or slave. To this end, you will find a jumper positioning table somewhere on the body of the drive unit.

1 7531	4321	
8642		

(7-8) (5-6) (3-4) (1-2)	
	Limit capacity to 32 Gbytes
	Master or single drive
	Drive is a slave
	Master with a non-ATA-compatible slave
	Enable cable select

Once this has been done, you are ready to install the drive/s.

Installing an ATA Drive

Hard drives are installed in the 3.5 inch drive bays at the bottom front of the system case.

1 Slide the drive into position

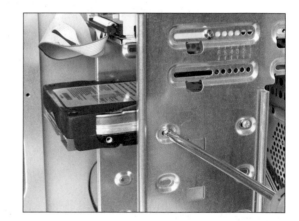

2 Secure the drive with the supplied screws

80-pin ATA interface cables are keyed to make sure they are fitted the right way round. If the plug won't fit one way, try it the other way.

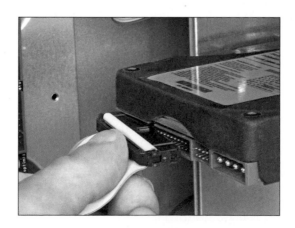

3 Connect the black end of the interface cable to the drive's socket

4 Connect the power supply

5 Locate the colored ATA socket on the motherboard

Hot tip

The motherboard will have two ATA sockets – one for the hard drive (colored) and one for the CD/DVD drive (black). Make sure you connect the drive to the correct colored socket.

119

6 Connect the other end of the interface cable to the motherboard ATA socket

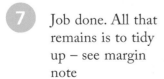

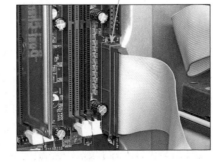

7 Job done. All that remains is to tidy up – see margin note

Hot tip

Don't leave the interface cable hanging loosely, this will obstruct airflow in the case. Fold up any slack and push it out of the way as far as possible.

Installing a Second ATA Drive

1 Slide the drive into the next but one bay from the main drive – see top margin note

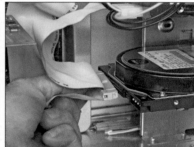

2 Secure the drive with the supplied screws

3 Connect the gray slave interface plug to the drive

4 Connect a power plug

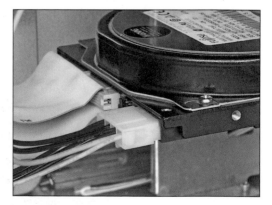

Installing a SATA Drive

This is exactly the same procedure as for an ATA drive. The only difference is that SATA drives use a different type of cable.

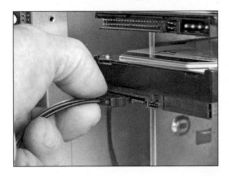

1 Connect one end of the power cable to the socket at the left of the drive

Hot tip

More recent PSUs built to the ATX12v V2.0 and V2.1 form factors provide a SATA power connection. Older PSUs do not, in which case a Molex adapter must be used, as shown left.

2 Connect the other end to a power plug – see margin note

3 Connect one end of the interface cable to the socket at the right of the power supply socket

Hot tip

The motherboard will provide two or more SATA sockets. These will be labeled SATA 1, SATA 2, etc. You can install as many drives as there are sockets.

4 Connect the other end to a SATA socket on the motherboard

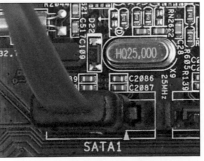

Installing a SATA Driver

Unlike ATA drives, which are ready to go once they have been partitioned and formatted, SATA drives require a driver to be installed first. This will usually be provided on a floppy disk by the motherboard manufacturer – see margin note.

Hot tip

Some motherboard manufacturers do not provide a floppy disk containing SATA drivers. If this is the case, you must make one yourself (instructions will be in the motherboard manual).

Typically, this involves booting the system from the motherboard disk and then simply following the prompts.

Note that this requires the CD drive to be set as the first boot device – see page 159.

Windows XP

With XP, installing a SATA driver is part of the XP installation procedure, so remember to set the CD drive as the first boot device as described on page 159. When you've done this, boot the PC with XP's installation disk in the CD drive.

When you see a message saying "Press any key to boot from CD....", do so.

Within the first minute of the installation, you will be prompted to press F6 to install RAID or SCSI drivers. After pressing the F6 key, the installation will continue. Shortly afterwards, you will see the following screen. Select the first option by pressing S.

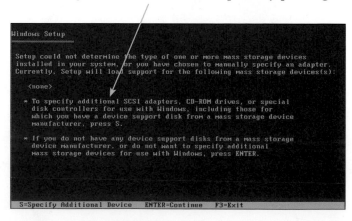

The next screen will ask you to insert the floppy disk. Do so and then press Enter. You'll see the following screen:

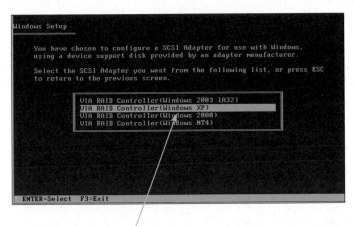

In the list of drivers, select the XP driver and press Enter. The driver will now be installed. At the next screen, just press Enter. XP's installation routine will now continue – see pages 160-161.

Windows Vista
The procedure is very similar to the one for XP. Run the Vista installation disk and when you see the "Where do you want to install Windows?" screen, click Load Driver.

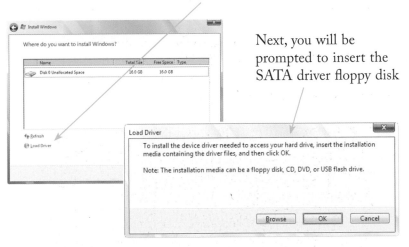

Next, you will be prompted to insert the SATA driver floppy disk

When you have inserted the disk, press OK. Then just follow the prompts. When the driver is loaded, start the Vista installation routine as described on pages 161-162.

Note that Windows Vista will install on a SATA drive without the SATA driver being loaded as described opposite, as Vista has native support for SATA. However, we recommend that you install the driver supplied by the motherboard manufacturer as this may give better results.

RAID Configurations

Very few people ever install two hard drives in their system, those who do will usually set them up in a master/slave relationship as described on page 117.

However, there is an alternative and this comes in the form of RAID (Redundant Array of Independent Disks). RAID is a way of configuring a combination of hard drives to gain specific benefits. Traditionally, it has been found in server and corporate environments where the need for the advantages it gives is greater.

Of the various RAID configurations, the ones described below may be of interest in a home-PC environment.

RAID 0

This requires a minimum of two drives, (preferably identical) and works by splitting (known as striping) the data equally between them. The result is much improved data transfer speeds as each drive handles part of a file.

RAID 1

This also requires a minimum of two drives. In this configuration, all data saved is duplicated (known as mirroring) on each drive. The purpose is data protection – if one drive fails, the data is recoverable from the other/s.

RAID 0+1

This is a combination of RAID 0 and RAID 1 and requires a minimum of four drives. Half the drives are used to stripe the data, and the other half to mirror it. Thus, it provides fast data transfer, together with data protection.

RAID 5

This requires a minimum of three drives. Data is striped across all the drives but an error checking bit (known as the parity bit) is also stored. Should any one drive fail, the RAID controller will calculate the missing data (using the parity bit) and keep the system running until the faulty drive can be replaced.

To implement RAID, you need a RAID controller, which sets up and maintains the configuration. Many motherboards now come with an integrated controller and if you are interested in RAID, we suggest you get one of these. Alternatively, you can add a PCI RAID controller card (shown left) to a board that doesn't.

Hot tip

If you are running Windows Vista, Windows 2000 or Windows XP Professional, it is possible to have a software RAID setup. This is controlled by the operating system.

There are, however, disadvantages. Software setups do have an adverse effect on general system performance and are not as efficient or reliable as hardware setups. For example, if the operating system should become corrupted, you could lose all your data.

124

PCI RAID Controller

11 Input Devices

In this chapter, we look at the ubiquitous mouse and the keyboard. Many people see these simple devices as not being worthy of too much attention, but they actually have a lot to offer.

Mouse Technology

Ball and Wheel

The original mouse design, ball and wheel, uses a mechanical system, whereby a rubber ball at the underside of the device operates a system of cogged wheels.

While perfectly functional, they have two inherent disadvantages: a) they are prone to dirt contamination via the ball that inhibits correct operation and b) they require the use of a mousemat.

Their only advantages are that they do not require a source of power and they are the cheapest type of mouse.

Optical (LED)

These devices use an LED, which projects light onto the work surface. Reflections of the light are picked up by an electronic sensor and translated by a chip into the data needed for positioning the pointer.

LED and electronic sensor on the underside of the mouse

The advantages of optical technology are: quicker and more precise operation, no moving parts to wear out and the ability to use the mouse on a range of surfaces without the need for a mousemat.

The disadvantages are that they cost a little more and require the use of batteries, which further adds to their cost in the long term.

The majority of today's mice are of the LED type.

Optical (Laser)

These mice have taken optical technology a step further by using a laser as the light source. This is able to read far more data, which together with other technical enhancements, results in a mouse that offers the highest levels of performance. For example, these devices can be used on any surface except glass.

Accordingly, laser technology is found only in professional mice intended for use by gamers, and high-end graphic applications. Not surprisingly, they are the most expensive type.

Hot tip

A big advantage of an optical mouse is that it can be used on most types of surfaces.

126

The MX 1000 laser mouse from Logitech

Mouse Specifications

As with all computer devices, the quality of a mouse is determined by its specifications. However, unlike most PC devices, for the vast majority of users, investigating it really isn't necessary as literally all the mice currently on the market are good enough for all but the most demanding applications.

The only ones who will need to do this are gamers and users of high-end graphic programs.

For those where only the best will do, the following specifications are the ones to be considered:

Don't forget

Unless you are in the market for a high-performance device or have a particular requirement, such as operating distance, mouse specifications as detailed on this page are not something you need to be overly concerned with.

Tracking Resolution

Tracking is defined as movement, and tracking resolution is the number of pixels that an optical sensor is able to recognize when the device is moved.

The higher the resolution, the more sensitive the mouse and thus, the less movement needed to obtain a response. Standard mice have a resolution of 400 to 800 dpi, while professional models will be up to 2500 dpi.

Tracking Speed

Tracking speed is the maximum speed that the mouse can be moved while still providing accurate tracking. Look for 40 inches per second with standard mice and 65 inches per second with professional mice.

Image Processing Rate

This is a measure of how many mega-pixels of data a mouse can assimilate in a second and determines its accuracy. The more data the mouse has, the more accurately it can position the pointer. Typical figures range from around 4.7 mega-pixels/sec for standard mice and up to 6.4 for professional models.

Acceleration

Mouse acceleration is how quickly the mouse responds to movement. Standard mice have figures of around 10 g (gravities), while professional mice can be as fast as 20 g.

Types of Mice

Wired

This is the traditional type of mouse and it uses a cord to connect to the PC. The advantage it has over its wireless cousins is that

the cord provides a faster and more reliable method of connection (although it must be said that there is not much in it, particularly in comparison to the high-performance laser mice).

Wireless

Wireless, or cordless, mice use radio frequency (RF) technology as the means of connecting to the PC. This does away with the need for a connecting cord and is their only real advantage.

Their main disadvantage is that a radio frequency connection can introduce a time lag between the user moving the mouse and movement of the pointer.

However, this delay is minute and should only be of concern to professional users (this is why many gamers will only use a wired mouse).

Trackball

A trackball is basically an up-ended mouse where the user positions the pointer by rotating the ball with a finger.

Apart from offering a high level of control, they are also ideal for those with hand or wrist disabilities, as they can be operated with a single finger.

Another advantage is that they can be used on any type of surface as the ball doesn't come into contact with it.

They do, however, take a bit of getting used to.

Beware

Make sure that your mouse uses FastRF wireless technology to minimize time lag. Standard RF technology is not so good in this respect. Also, be aware that even FastRF is only effective at up to six feet from the PC. Use the mouse at a greater distance than this and time lag may be introduced.

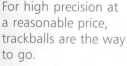

Hot tip

For high precision at a reasonable price, trackballs are the way to go.

Mouse Features

To enable the user to get the best out of a mouse, it must provide suitable features and controls, particularly if it is designed for professional use. The following are what you should be looking for.

Programmable Buttons

These allow the user to map different functions to a button, such as close, open, zoom, etc and allow the user to do much more with the mouse.

Basic mice will come with one left-click button, one right-click button and a center scroll wheel, which may also double as a programmable button. Better models will have three or four programmable buttons, while professional models will have up to eight. Professional mice may also have a tilting scroll wheel, which allows horizontal scrolling.

Batteries

A well used optical mouse will go through batteries at a surprising rate, thus adding considerably to its initial cost. Using rechargeables is the best way to minimize this, but good ones are expensive.

Cheap mice will be provided with either no batteries at all, or two standard AA batteries. Factor in the cost of four rechargeables (two in use, two recharging) and the mouse is no longer cheap. So look for a model that provides rechargeables in the box – four, ideally.

Also, consider the type of rechargeables supplied (or bought). Standard nickel cadmium batteries (Ni-Cad) do not last nearly as long as high-capacity Nickel-Metal Hydride (Ni-MH) batteries.

Professional models come with a built-in battery pack and a charging station (shown right), into which you place the device when it's not in use. This keeps it fully charged at all times. A battery life LED indicator is a useful feature to look out for.

Software

Most mice these days come with control panel software that allows you to configure basic functions, such as pointer options, button mapping, etc. The software supplied with better models provide many more options that allow you to customize the mouse to suit particular applications. Some high-end mice allow you to change some settings, e.g. screen resolution, at the click of a button (handy for gamers).

Hot tip

Optical mice, typically, have an operating range of about six feet, which allows you to sit further back from the display.

If you need more than this, consider going for a Bluetooth mouse. This provides an operating range of 30 feet or more (you will of course have to add a Bluetooth adapter to the PC).

Keyboard Technology

Keyboards are simple devices that basically comprise a switching system, LED lights, and a processor to convert the keystrokes to signals that can be interpreted by the PC.

As all types of keyboard have lights and a processor, the main differentiating factor between them is the switching technology used. The most common types are discussed below.

Capacitive

In a capacitive keyboard, each key has its own circuit. When the key is depressed, the capacitance (electrical charge) in the circuit is altered. The change is then translated by the processor. Essentially, it is a non-mechanical system and as a result, it is the most durable type of keyboard. These devices also have an extremely tactile key action.

Note that capacitive keyboards are very expensive and will be available only from specialist manufacturers.

Mechanical

Next in terms of quality is the mechanical type of keyboard. These devices use a mechanical switch for each key. They also employ a feedback mechanism that produces a tactile "clicky" feel to the key action. In addition, the switches are usually of the self-cleaning variety, which means that they provide good long-term performance.

As with the capacitive type, these keyboards are not commonly available, so you may need to visit a specialist manufacturer.

Membrane

In a membrane keyboard, none of the keys has an individual switch or circuit; instead, they all sit on a sheet of plastic (the membrane). This is imprinted with a metallic pattern that when touched by a depressed key, acts like a switch and sends the "key depressed" signal to the computer.

These keyboards are much cheaper as they have many less parts inside them. However, they do have the disadvantages of poor durability, and a spongy, non-tactile feel to the key action.

The standard keyboards supplied with PC systems and by PC parts vendors are of the membrane type.

Don't forget

Capacitive and mechanical keyboards are the best choice for professional use. Membrane models are fine for general purpose use.

Beware

Touch typists will not get on with a membrane keyboard – their key action is not positive enough.

Types of Keyboard

Rather than settle for the cheap keyboards typically supplied by PC manufacturers, the self-builder has a range to choose from, many of which are designed with specific purposes in mind.

Professional

High-quality keyboards use either a mechanical or capacitive key system as opposed to the membrane system used by cheaper models. For touch typists, they are the best option by far.

Ergonomic

Also intended for the serious typist are the ergonomically designed keyboards. While these take a bit of getting used to, they do make typing a more speedy and comfortable process.

They are constructed in a way that allows users to hold their hands in a more comfortable, slightly angled, position while

typing. This can also help prevent or alleviate Carpal Tunnel Syndrome; an affliction that affects the wrists.

Taking the concept a bit further are split keyboards that have an adjustable hinge in the middle to vary the angle at which the keys are presented to the user's hands.

Program Specific

Some keyboards provide keys that are relevant to specific applications. For example, those of you who frequently use Microsoft Office applications can buy models that have keys relevant to Word, PowerPoint, Excel, etc.

Image reprinted with permission from ViewSonic Corporation

Others have keys that control multimedia functions such as play and pause, Internet and email functions.

131

Hot tip

Also available for serious typists is the Dvorak keyboard. These use a different key layout that is considered to be more efficient than the QWERTY layout found on standard keyboards.

Hot tip

Those of you always on the move might like to take their keyboard with them. This is easy with a roll-up keyboard. Made of a thin pliant material such as silicon, you simply roll it up and stuff it in a bag. These devices are very thin and weigh only a few ounces.

...cont'd

Gaming Keyboards

For some game genres, keyboards are the best type of controller, e.g. strategy games, such as Microsoft's Age of Empires, where the game action is controlled by the keyboard.

While standard keyboards are adequate, much better results will be had from one of the specialized gaming keyboards.

Don't forget

If you play strategy games, a keyboard will be the best type of controller. A gaming keyboard will provide many more options than a standard one.

These have a multitude of programmable keys and allows the user to customize them to suit specific games. Most also have an integral joystick, plus illuminated keys that allow games to be played in the dark (hardly essential, but cool nevertheless).

One of the most important features that they offer to gamers, is the ability to set up macro commands that combine multiple keystrokes into one. For example, with a standard keyboard, getting a game character to jump forward and kick-out simultaneously will require three keys to be pressed at the same time. A gaming keyboard will do this with one keystroke.

Doom 3 keyset from Ideazon

You can also find keyboards tailored for specific games. Take a look at Ideazon's website at www.zboard.com. Here you will find a range of keysets designed for use with games such as Doom 3, Medal of Honor and EverQuest 2.

Don't forget

Ideazon's Z-Board features a base unit that can be customized with a wide range of interchangeable keysets.

Wireless Keyboards

These are becoming increasingly popular as they reduce the amount of clutter on the desktop. They also allow the user to sit a lot further back from the monitor, thus reducing eyestrain.

These keyboards are very expensive though, and cost five or six times as much as a standard model.

Keyboard Specifications

Important keyboard specifications include:

Switching Technology

There are quite a few methods used but the most common are capacitive, mechanical and membrane, as explained on page 130.

Users who do a lot of intensive typing should look at capacitive and mechanical models. All other users will be fine with the membrane type.

Keystrokes

This specification relates to the expected lifespan of the switching technology used by a keyboard.

Capacitive types offer the highest rating – 20 to 50 million keystrokes, while mechanical switching ratings are, typically, around the 20 million mark. Membrane switching is the least durable and varies from 5 to 10 million keystrokes.

Note that a few high-end membrane keyboards offer a keystroke rating of up to 50 million. However, while they may be as durable, they will not be as pleasant to use as capacitive and mechanical types.

Interface

Nearly all keyboards these days use the USB interface. However, it is a fact that the traditional PS/2 keyboard interface is still perfectly adequate for the low bandwidth requirements of any current keyboard.

Therefore, those of you who would rather keep your USB ports for other devices that will benefit from the higher speed USB offers, should consider getting a keyboard that uses the PS/2 port. Note that some keyboards can run from either and will be supplied with a USB to PS/2 adapter.

If you go for a wireless model, be aware of the issue of time lag as explained on page 128; this applies equally to keyboards. Go for one that uses FastRF technology.

Peak Tactile Force

This is the measure of how tactile the key action is and a good figure is 60 to 70 Grams.

Hot tip

A recent technology employs laser beams to create a virtual keyboard. A device about the size of a cigarette lighter attaches to the PC and projects an image of a full-sized keyboard onto the work surface. It also provides realistic keystroke sounds.

Keyboard Features

As with the mouse, a basic keyboard, typically available for $7 or so, is functional but will provide nothing in the way of extras. A more fully-featured model can enhance your work in a number of ways. Lets look at some useful examples:

Key Functions

Many keyboards come with a small software program that allows the user to map specific functions to certain keys (usually the F keys). This provides very useful shortcuts that can open web pages and applications with a single keystroke.

Spill Resistance

As many users will testify, it's all too easy to knock a drink over and into the keyboard. Even if this does no permanent damage, in the case of sugary beverages, it may be necessary to remove the key caps to clean away the sticky residue.

Much easier then, to buy a model that is spill resistant. These are designed in such a way that liquids simply pass through the keyboard and can then be drained away through holes at the bottom of the case.

Ergonomic Adjustments

Extended periods of keyboard use can be very tiring on the wrists and fingers and can lead to repetitive stress injuries. Avoid the potential for this by buying a model that features an adjustable typing angle and wrist rest.

Lighting

Backlit keys will be useful when typing in low-light conditions. It can also be an aesthetic feature.

Integrated Pointing Devices

Compactly designed keyboards are available that feature a built-in trackball mouse or touch pad.

These keyboards are useful when working in cramped conditions that do not allow enough room for using a separate mouse.

Hot tip

Cheap keyboards have the characters printed on the keycaps and eventually they will wear off. Look for a model that has the characters etched on to the keys.

134

Hot tip

Gaming keyboards include features not found on standard models. For example: a backlit LCD panel that displays system information such as CPU and memory utilization.

12 Sound Systems

For most users, integrated sound is quite adequate; we look at the reasons for this. Other users, however, such as gamers and musicians, will need a dedicated sound card. Read on to see why.

Overview

Sound is one of the less important aspects of a computer, as for most tasks, it simply isn't needed. That said, there are probably very few people who would opt to do without it completely as it does add another element to computing. For gamers it is essential.

Hot tip

For the self-builder working to a budget, the computer's sound system offers an opportunity to cut costs. Unless there is a specific need for any of the features provided by a dedicated sound card, an integrated sound system will fit the bill nicely.

Beware

When buying a high-quality sound card, you will also need to factor in the price of a set of high-quality speakers. These can cost as much as the card itself, and so the setup as a whole can turn out to be very expensive.

Most people find the sound systems integrated into the majority of motherboards to be more than adequate for all their sound requirements.

For those who want high-quality sound reproduction, or musicians who need music-mastering facilities, the issue is more complicated, as a top-end sound card will be required. These come with bewildering sets of specifications, features and sockets, and require a bit of homework to ensure the correct choice is made.

For the self-builder who is working to a budget, the high cost of top-end sound cards also needs to be considered as these can cost even more than video cards.

However, for most people, a computer's sound system is an area in which economies can be made with very little penalty in terms of functionality or performance.

Integrated Sound Systems

In the past, the vast majority of computers were supplied with two nasty little speakers, which were good for reproducing the operating system's clicks, jingles and little else. The integrated sound systems supplied with these PCs were equally basic.

Thankfully, the situation is rather different today, and most of the motherboards currently on the market come with quite sophisticated sound systems that can be good enough even for the gamer. It is quite common now to find systems offering seven-channel 5.1 surround sound that can take advantage of multi-speaker setups.

Integrated sound systems do not require the use of a PCI slot as do sound cards. This gives you more room for expansion in other areas.

One drawback is that they rely on the PC's CPU and memory to do the number-crunching, thus reducing overall system performance. In addition, they provide less in the way of input and output sockets than sound cards do, which can be restrictive.

This motherboard may offer seven-channel 5.1 surround sound but it does not supply all the necessary outputs. This means messing about with software settings to get all the speakers working

Also, good as they are, they still do not provide the kind of high-fidelity required by the music purist, nor do they offer anything to the musician in the way of authoring features.

If you do decide to take the integrated route, take a look at the specifications as there are still systems around which are not so good. Basically, the more features offered, the better the performance will be. Look for things such as support for DirectX, EAX, DirectSound 3D and multi-channel speaker systems.

Don't forget

As with integrated video, integrated sound systems have their pros and cons.

Advantages are:
• No cost
• No PCI slot used
• No hardware to be installed

Disadvantages are:
• Slight degradation of overall system performance
• Performance levels, while adequate, do not match those offered by dedicated sound cards
• Limited features
• Limited input & output sockets

137

Hot tip

If you intend to use a multi-channel integrated sound system, check that the motherboard provides the necessary output sockets – not all do.

Sound Cards

People who need to buy a dedicated sound card will fall into one of the following categories:

- Speed aficionados who don't want to sacrifice even the small hit in performance that integrated sound will make on their system

- Musicians who need specific mastering functions such as Wave Table Synthesis support

- Gamers who want to get the maximum sound effects from their games

- Music buffs who require the highest possible quality of sound reproduction

Budget Sound Cards

If you are looking to make your system as fast as possible, then integrated sound is out due to the demands it makes on the system's CPU and memory. While the drop in performance is relatively slight, it is, nevertheless, there.

In this situation, a low- to mid-level sound card should suffice, as all you are looking for is something to take the load off the CPU and memory. Anything else it offers is a bonus.

However, you should be aware that some of the really low-end cards actually pass the number-crunching on to the system's CPU, which means that essentially they are no better than integrated sound systems. About the only benefit you may get from one of these cards is better connectivity by way of the number of input and output ports. So check the specifications.

As a general rule, we would advise you not to bother with budget sound cards at all. As already mentioned, very often they are no better than integrated systems; they may, in fact, be even less capable.

Spend a bit more to get a mid-range card, such as the SoundBlaster Live (shown right) from Creative.

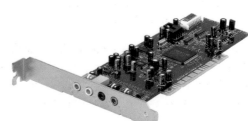

Sound Cards for Gamers

Gamers who are not satisfied with the quality of integrated sound need to look at several aspects of sound cards before buying one.

The first point to note is that the fidelity of a sound card's output will be of less importance to the gamer than its ability to create the illusion of being in the middle of the action. For example, if a game character walks behind you, his footsteps should sound as though they are coming from over your shoulder.

To be able to do this, the sound card must provide the following:

- Multiple speaker support – each pair of speakers requires a line-out socket. So a five- or six-speaker system will require three of these, and a seven- or eight-speaker system will require four

- 3D Surround Sound – also known as Positional Audio, this technology accurately recreates the relative positioning of sound in a three-dimensional environment. There are various versions, but the de facto standard is currently Creative's EAX. Sensuara's 3DPA is another popular one

Also important is the number of simultaneous sounds the card can process (these are referred to as channels [see margin note] in the specifications). If the application throws more of these at the sound card than it is designed to handle, the system's CPU has to help out. If this happens when playing a game, the game's frame rate may be adversely affected.

Thirty-two channels is a reasonable starting point; anything higher is better.

The more APIs (application program interfaces) the card supports, the better. These allow the game to communicate with the sound card and different types of sound use specific APIs. If they are not supported by the card then you will be missing out on some of the game's sound effects.

The gamer might also want to look at the specifications that determine the quality of the sound card's output. Having just saved the world from marauding aliens, he may need to chill-out by listening to a nice piano concerto.

Hot tip

DirectX support is just as important for a sound card as it is for a video card. Make sure the card supports the latest version.

Hot tip

When applied to a sound card, the term "channel" has two meanings:

1) The number of speakers that can be connected to the card. A card with one output jack will be able to support two channels; each channel supporting one speaker – one left, one right. If it has two jacks, it will support four speakers, and so on

2) The number of simultaneous sounds the card can process by itself

...cont'd

High-Fidelity Sound Cards

Music buffs who like to listen to crystal clear audio need to investigate a different set of specifications. 3D Surround Sound will be less important than the fidelity of the sound card's output.

This is indicated by the following specifications:

● Bit-Depth – this indicates how much of the original sound file is reproduced by the card. High bit-depth means high-fidelity and dynamic range

● Signal-to-Noise Ratio (SNR) – this is a measure of how "clean" a sound signal is. The higher the amount of background noise (electrical interference, etc), the lower the signal-to-noise ratio

● Total Harmonic Distortion (THD) – this is a measurement of the noise produced by the sound card itself during the process of converting the analog signal to a digital signal

● Frequency Response (FR) – this is the range of frequencies that the sound card can recognise and is specified in upper and lower limits

● Sampling Rate (SR) – this determines the range of frequencies that can be converted to digital format by the sound card, and thus the accuracy of the reproduction

Taken as a whole, these five specifications are the measure of a sound card's output quality.

The figures in the table below show what to expect from low-end, mid-range and top-end sound cards.

	Low-End	Mid-Range	Top-End
Bit-Depth	16-bits	16-bits	24-bits
SNR	75 Db	90 Db	115 Db
THD	0.5 %	0.05 %	0.01 %
FR	20 Hz-20 KHz	20 Hz-20 KHz	15 Hz-40 KHz
SR	48 KHz	48 KHz	96 KHz

Sound Cards For Musicians

In addition to the specifications discussed on page 140, those interested in creating music on their PCs also need to consider the features provided by the card.

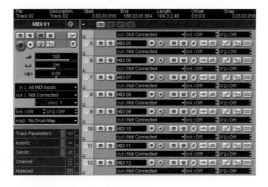

These will include balanced analog inputs/outputs, digital inputs/outputs in AES/EBU or S/PDIF formats, full duplex and dedicated wave-mixers.

Used in conjunction with a suitable mastering application, such as Steinberg's Cubase, a card offering these features will turn a PC into a very capable recording studio.

Whatever type of card you go for, be aware that these devices are prone to picking up electrical interference (noise) from other parts in the system. This manifests itself as humming, hissing, clicks, etc. While good quality sound cards include circuitry to minimize this, it is unlikely to be eliminated completely.

So if you want as clean a signal as possible, buy a card that includes a break-out box as shown below. This either sits on the desktop or can be installed in a spare drive bay, and houses the input/output jacks and the audio converters.

This type of arrangement eliminates the issue of electrical noise by converting the analog signal to digital form *before* it is sent to the card in the PC where noise will be induced from nearby parts, such as the hard drive and other expansion cards.

Hot tip

Do not overlook the "connectivity" of the sound card. The more inputs and outputs it has, the more you will be able to do with it, e.g. microphone recording, the attachment of multiple-speaker systems, digital audio devices and other electronic equipment such as a stereo system.

141

Don't forget

For high-quality sound output look for a sound card that is supplied with a separate break-out box.

Installing a Sound Card

Install the sound card as you would any other expansion card. However, don't forget the issue of electrical interference from other system devices, as explained on page 141.

If your card is supplied with a break-out box, this will not be a problem. If it's not, minimize interference as much as possible by situating the card as far from other devices as you can. This is demonstrated below.

1 Sound card fitted well away from other devices

Don't forget

Don't forget to connect the 4-pin analog cable to the CD drive (if there is one).

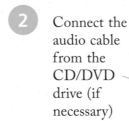

2 Connect the audio cable from the CD/DVD drive (if necessary)

3 Secure the backplate to the chassis

13 Removable Media Drives

One of the biggest boons for PC users in recent years has been the introduction of writable CD and DVD drives. This chapter shows you what is available, explains all the various CD and DVD formats and shows how to pick the drive best suited to your needs.

What's Available?

Given the enormous storage capacities offered by today's removable media drives, no self-respecting system can possibly be without one. The uses for the discs are endless – movie and music recording, system backups, data transfer between PCs, etc. The problem is choosing the right type of drive and format.

Do you settle for a basic CD drive or do you splash out for a DVD drive? If you do buy a DVD model, which format do you go for – DVD-ROM, DVD+, DVD- or DVD-RAM.

Hot tip

The simplest way to avoid the issue of which type of drive to buy with regard to format compatibility, is to buy a multi-function drive.

These are compatible with all the current CD/DVD disc formats. They do cost more though.

Then there is the humble floppy drive. In terms of storage capacity, floppy disks offer a measly 1.44 MB, compared to 650 MB for a CD and up to 8.5 GB for a dual-layer DVD disc. Are they worth buying at all?

Some drives, known as multi-function drives, can handle both CDs and DVDs. A slightly different option are the Zip and Rev drives from Iomega. These use magnetic disk media and work in the same way as a hard drive does.

Your choices are:

Hot tip

Used in conjunction with a suitable backup utility, such as Powerquest's Drive Image, high-capacity CDs/DVDs enable you to make a complete backup of your system.

- Floppy drives

- CD drives

- DVD drives

- Zip/Rev drives

Floppy Drives

While these devices are painfully slow and the disks hold a pitiful amount of data (1.44 MB) by today's standards, they are, nevertheless, still useful in many ways. Some typical applications are:

- Small hardware drivers (mice, keyboards, SATA, etc)

- BIOS flash upgrades

- Rescue disks

- Text documents (one disk will hold a full length novel)

Floppy disks are rugged in construction compared to CDs and are easily slipped into a pocket. Also, virtually all system cases come with a 3.5 inch floppy drive bay. So, given that these devices cost next to nothing, you may as well have one.

A useful feature provided with some current models is a built-in flash card reader.

This enables the drive to read, and transfer to the hard drive, the contents of various types of flash memory. For example: Compact Flash, MicroDrive, MemoryStick, SmartMedia, MultiMedia and Secure Digital Cards.

Another related option is to buy one of the Superdisk drives. These devices use disks that have capacities up to 250 MB, although the disks are more expensive than a floppy disk. These drives are also compatible with standard 1.44 MB floppies.

A further boon is that many of them provide a formatting system that can increase the storage capacity of a floppy disk to a comparatively whopping 32 MB. With one of these devices, that pile of redundant floppies that most PC users have lying about will suddenly take on a new lease of life.

145

CD-ROM Drives

For your new computer, the very minimum you will want in terms of CD capabilities is a CD-ROM drive. These devices are read-only, which means that you can access the data on the disc but you cannot write anything to it.

If you have no need for CD writing, one of these drives will be the least expensive option for your PC and they are available for little more than the cost of a floppy drive.

CD Writers

Also known as "burners" as the writing process involves literally burning the data to the disc, these devices are a step up from CD-ROM drives. Not only can they read CDs, they can also write to them. They come in two types – CD-R and CD-RW.

CD-R
A CD-R (writer) drive will record to a "write-once-only" disc, known as a CD-R disc. Once these discs have been used, they cannot be used again. Note that CD-R discs are the most common type as they are cheap, quick to write to and have a longer expected shelf-life than CD-RW discs. Due to differences in their composition they are also considered to be more reliable, i.e. there is less chance of data corruption.

CD-RW
CD-RW (re-writer) drives will record to CD-R discs and also to CD-RW (re-writeable) discs. They are no different to CD-R drives apart from their ability to record to a re-writable disc.

The only real advantage CD-RW discs hold over CD-Rs is the fact they can be reused – about a thousand times according to the manufacturers (as with all manufacturer claims though, this needs to be taken with a pinch of salt).

In practice, there are very few CD-R drives around now – virtually all CD writers are re-writers.

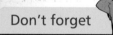

Don't forget

CD-R discs can be recorded to only once. However, they are cheap, quick and reliable.

CD-RW discs, on the other hand, can be reused a number of times. They do cost more though. In addition, recording to them can take considerably longer than with CD-R discs.

For long-term data storage, always use CD-R discs.

DVD Drives

DVD (Digital Versatile Disc) drives are very similar in concept to CD drives. The basic difference is that DVD drives use a much narrower laser for reading and writing, this allows more tracks to be squeezed onto the discs. Thus vastly increasing their storage capacity.

In addition, the composition of a DVD disc allows two layers of data on each side, giving a theoretical maximum of some 17 GB. In practice though, most DVD discs currently on sale have a capacity of 4.7 GB, with 8.5 GB (dual-layer) versions becoming increasingly common.

Don't forget

DVD discs are available in a dual-layer format, which nearly doubles their storage capacity.

Due to their huge storage capacity, DVD discs are used for commercially produced movies, as an entire movie can be stored on one disc. This capacity is also beginning to be utilized by the PC industry. For example, Microsoft's Encarta Reference Library, which requires five CDs, is available on a single DVD. With the ever increasing size of software applications, you can expect to see many more of them shipped on DVD discs in the near future. This is one reason to buy a DVD drive.

The high capacity of DVD discs is handy for PC users as well. Typical applications are large-scale system backups and the storage of video, such as TV shows recorded via TV tuner devices.

Another plus for these drives is the fact that they can also read CDs (both software CDs and writable CDs); this makes them the most versatile type of optical drive presently available.

DVD drives are available in three versions: read-only, writable and re-writable. The decision of which type to go for is based on the same reasons for choosing between the various types of CD drives.

Hot tip

If you want to watch commercial movies on your PC, you will need a DVD drive.

DVD Formats

The issue of DVD formats also needs to be considered. Currently, there are four of these.

DVD-ROM

Similar to a CD-ROM, discs in this format can only be read – they cannot be written to.

DVD-

This format is supported by Panasonic, Toshiba, Apple, Hitachi, NEC, Pioneer, Samsung and Sharp. It is available in write-once versions (DVD-R) and rewrite versions (DVD-RW).

DVD+

A more recent format, DVD+ is supported by Philips, Sony, Hewlett-Packard, Dell, Ricoh and others. As with DVD-, write-once (DVD+R) and rewrite (DVD+RW) versions are available.

DVD-RAM

A DVD-RAM disc is very similar to a hard drive in the way it is used. This format also offers faster data access, and higher levels of reliability than the + and - formats. However, DVD-RAM discs can be read only in a DVD-RAM drive – the format is not generally compatible with DVD+ and DVD- drives.

The table below summarizes the pros and cons of the formats:

Hot tip

If your primary purpose for buying a DVD drive is long-term data storage, consider one of the DVD-RAM drives. DVD-RAM discs have the highest life expectancy of all the formats. Furthermore, the drives themselves provide data protection facilities, e.g. the marking of bad sectors. These features make DVD-RAM the most reliable format.

Don't forget

The DVD+ format is more advanced than DVD-. It offers faster write speeds, slightly higher disc capacity, and built-in data correction. However, DVD+ discs are more expensive than DVD- and the format is generally considered to be less compatible with home and car DVD players.

Disc	Uses	Pros	Cons
DVD-ROM	Commercial movies, PC games, software	Plays on all drives	Cannot be recorded to
DVD-RAM	Data backup	Offers hard drive like operation, and fast data access. Most reliable format	Poor compatibility. Cannot be played on home DVD players. Discs are expensive
DVD-	Good for video and audio discs, general data backup and transfer	High level of compatibility with other formats and home DVD players	Lower maximum capacity than DVD+ discs. Write/read speeds are slower than DVD+
DVD+	Good for mixed data discs. Can also be used for video and audio discs	Good level of compatibility with home DVD players	Compatibility with other formats and home DVD players lower than DVD-

CD/DVD Drive Specifications

Having decided what type of drive/format you want, the next step is to take a closer look at these devices and see what they actually offer. The following specifications are the ones that should be considered.

Interface

The vast majority of drives currently on the market use the ATA interface (with an extension known as ATAPI). They are also available with USB, FireWire, SCSI and SATA interfaces, which all offer *potentially* faster data transfer rates – see top margin note.

Read/Write Speeds

The speed at which a drive reads and writes is indicated by x ratings in the specifications. Usually, these are also marked prominently on the packaging, as shown below.

Hot tip

The interface used by the drive is something that you don't need to worry about unless you are looking to "future-proof" your system. The ATAPI interface, which is used by most drives, is quite capable of running the drives currently on the market at their full potential.

Using this as a typical example, the first figure, 40x, is the speed at which the drive writes to a CD-R.

The second, 12x, is the speed at which it writes to a CD-RW, and the third figure, 48x, is its read speed.

However, for these figures to have any meaning, you need to know what the x represents. In the case of CD drives, it represents 150 KB/s. So the CD drive in our example above, has a CD-R write speed of 6.0 MB/s (150 x 40).

DVD drives also use this convention. You will notice though, that the x ratings are much lower, typically 16x, 4x and 16x. On the face of it, this would seem to indicate that DVD drives are slower than CD drives.

However, they are actually much faster, this is because the x represents 1.32 MB/s (as opposed to 150 KB/s with CD drives). So a 16x rating indicates a write speed of 21 MB/s – three and a half times as fast as a CD writer.

Don't forget

The lower x ratings of DVD drives does not mean that these drives are slower than CD drives. They read data just as quickly and actually write data considerably faster.

...cont'd

Writing Mode

A very important factor in the performance of an optical drive is the maintenance of a constant data transfer rate across the entire disc. To achieve this, manufacturers use one of three methods: Constant Linear Velocity (CLV), Zoned Constant Linear Velocity (ZCLV) and Constant Angular Velocity (CAV).

All you need to know here is that budget and mid-range drives use the CLV or ZCLV method, while top-end models use CAV.

Access Time

This is the time needed to locate a specific item of data on the disc. This metric is measured in milliseconds and you should look for a figure no higher than 100 ms.

Buffer Size

Optical drives use a buffer to ensure that data flows to the disc smoothly and without interruption during the writing process; this helps to eliminate errors. Typically, drives are supplied with a 2 MB buffer and this is the minimum that you should accept. High-quality drives can have buffers as large as 8 MB.

Recommended Media

The build quality of CDs and DVDs varies widely and some drives have trouble with low-quality discs. To enable users to avoid this potential problem, most manufacturers provide a list of media recommended for use with their drives, as shown below:

Recommended Media		(All DVD-RW and CD-RW media is rewritable up to 1,000 times)
DVD+R	16X	Taiyo Yuden, Verbatim/Mitsubishi
	8X, 4X	Maxell, Ricoh, Taiyo Yuden, Verbatim/Mitsubishi
DVD+RW	4X	Ricoh, Verbatim/Mitsubishi
DVD+R DL	8X, 4X	Verbatim/Mitsubishi
DVD-R	16X, 8X, 4X	Maxell, Taiyo Yuden, TDK, Verbatim/Mitsubishi
DVD-RW	4X, 2X	TDK, Verbatim/Mitsubishi
DVD-R DL	4X	Verbatim/Mitsubishi, Victor
CD-R	48X	Maxell, Taiyo Yuden, TDK
	40X	Ricoh
CD-RW	32X, 24X	Verbatim/Mitsubishi
	10X, 4X	Ricoh, Verbatim/Mitsubishi Chemical

Dual-Layer Technology

This is the latest DVD innovation and it doubles the maximum storage capacity of a DVD to 8.5 GB. However, dual-layer discs can only be written and read by a dual-layer drive. Also, 8.5 GB dual-layer discs currently cost three times as much as a single-layer 4.7 GB disc, which makes them poor value for money.

Hot tip

If you already have a collection of written discs, it is worth making sure that the drive you buy will be able to read them. Check the manufacturer's Recommended Media list.

Beware

If you are tempted by the high storage capacities offered by dual-layer DVDs, remember that they will be an expensive way of archiving your data.

Beyond DVD

At the time of writing, the next generation of high-capacity optical disc drives is about to hit the market. So although it's a relative newcomer, the end is already in sight for DVD.

However, it's a cloudy issue at the moment as there are two competing standards – Blu-ray and HD-DVD. The situation is very similar to the video recorder format war between VHS and Betamax a few years ago.

What's on offer then? In a nutshell, huge storage capacity. Blu-ray discs can hold 25 GB (50 GB with dual-layer) of data, and HD-DVD 15 GB (30 GB with dual-layer). Future generation discs are expected to hold up to 200 GB.

Why the need for all this capacity? The arrival of High-Definition TV (HD-TV) is the answer.

Discs offering this level of capacity will be able to hold two hours of high-definition video, enough for a full-length movie.

The potential commercial benefits for the movie studios and related industries are enormous.

Hot tip

Both types of drive are able to read current generation DVDs and CDs.

As far as PC users are concerned, apart from being able to watch movies, either format takes data storage options to a completely different level. For example, you will probably be able to backup your entire system on a single disc.

So if you have the need, and a deep pocket, go for it. As to which format is going to emerge triumphant, you will need a crystal ball to predict this.

Whichever it is, as with the first generation of DVD players and media, they are both going to be extremely expensive initially. So our advice is to wait and see how it all pans out or at least until prices drop to an affordable level.

Zip/Rev Drives

While you are going to need a CD or DVD drive in your system, with regard to data storage they do have some drawbacks. The main one is that the writing process requires the use of a third-party program. Also, they are not as intuitive as a hard drive – you cannot "drag & drop", or save to a disc from a program's file menu, for example.

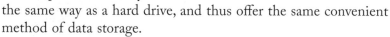

Enter the Zip and Rev drives from Iomega. Available in internal and external models, these drives operate in exactly the same way as a hard drive, and thus offer the same convenient method of data storage.

Basically, they are a turbo-charged version of the floppy disk drive. The differences lie in the speed at which they operate, the level of storage capacity offered and the range of features and options provided. Advantages over CD/DVD drives include:

- Data transfer speeds are much higher

- The disks are housed in a tough plastic case, which makes them less susceptible to physical damage

- They provide a range of features, such as password protection and an integrated backup facility

- Rev drive disks provide much higher storage capacity

Disks for Zip drives are available in capacities of 100, 250 and 750 MB. Rev disks provide a massive 35 or 70 GB of storage.

The latter is intended for users who have large-scale backup requirements. In operation, it has data transfer speeds similar to a hard drive and thus, provides one of the best backup solutions currently on the market.

The only drawback with these drives is the cost of the media: a single 250 MB Zip disk costs approximately $10, while a 70 GB Rev disk costs some $65. If you buy them in packs, though, the cost does come down.

Hot tip

Zip drives are the perfect solution for people who need a quick and flexible means of storing small amounts of data.

Don't forget

A feature offered by Zip and Rev drives that may be useful to some users is password protection.

Beware

Media for Zip and Rev drives are very expensive on a cost/capacity ratio in comparison to other types of storage media.

Installing a Floppy Drive

The floppy drive fits at the top of the 3.5 inch drive bay assembly (above the hard drive). Install it as follows:

1 Slide the drive along the supporting shelves until the front is lined up with the front aperture. Then screw it into place

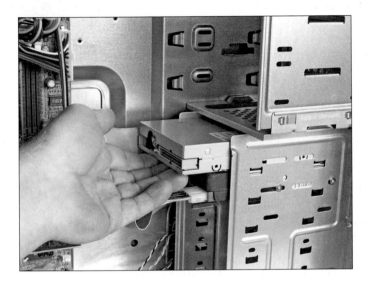

2 Connect the power plug to the socket at the left of the drive

Don't forget

The floppy drive's power is supplied by the small 4-pin connector shown below. This is the smallest of the PSU's power connectors.

...cont'd

Next, take a look at the interface cable. This will have a red stripe on one side and also, a twist in the middle at one end. The connector next to the twist goes to the drive, with the red stripe on the left-hand side. The other end goes to the motherboard, again with the stripe on the left-hand side. This is demonstrated below:

3 The drive connection with the twist next to the connector

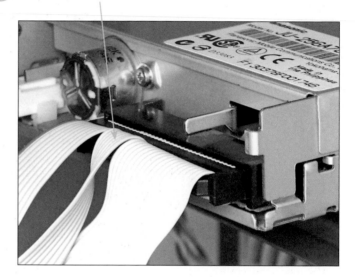

4 The motherboard connector with the red stripe on the left

Installing a CD/DVD Drive

1 Remove the front panel of the system case and then remove the appropriate blanking plate

2 Insert the drive from the front (if you try doing it from the back, the PSU will block access) and screw it in place

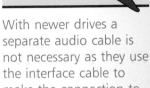

Hot tip

With newer drives a separate audio cable is not necessary as they use the interface cable to make the connection to the sound system. These drives use a technology called Digital Audio Extraction (DAE).

3 If the drive has an audio cable (see top margin note) to connect it to the sound system, plug one end in the socket at the far left

Don't forget

80-pin interface cables are keyed to make sure they fit correctly. However, the older 40-pin cables are not, so it is possible to fit these the wrong way. If this is what you are using, keep the striped edge on the right.

4 Keeping the striped edge to the right, plug the interface cable into the drive

...cont'd

5　Connect the power supply plug

Hot tip

You may need to consult the motherboard or sound card documentation to see where to connect the audio cable.

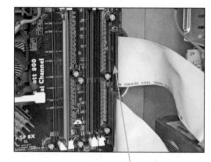 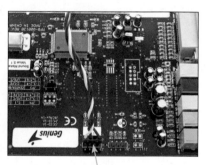

6　Connect the drive to the black ATA socket on the motherboard

7　Connect the audio cable (if necessary) to the sound system

Don't forget

In the case of a second drive, you must set it as the slave. The jumper settings are stamped on the casing at the rear.

If you decide to install a second drive, perhaps a DVD model to complement a CD drive, the first step is to set it as the slave; as shown right.

Then at step 4 (on the previous page), plug the slave connector (as shown on page 120, step 3) into the drive. Otherwise, the procedure is exactly the same.

14 Setting Up the System

This chapter shows how to complete your new PC by setting up hardware devices, enabling USB, installing the operating system and installing hardware drivers.

Navigating the BIOS

The final stage of building your PC includes configuring some hardware devices in the BIOS. To access the BIOS setup program, you need to press a key as the PC starts – see top margin note.

When the BIOS program opens, you will see the following screen – see bottom margin note.

Hot tip

The key required to enter the BIOS setup program varies from system to system, but is usually DEL with AWARD BIOSs and F2 with AMI BIOSs. It is usually specified on the first boot screen but if it isn't, details will be in the motherboard manual.

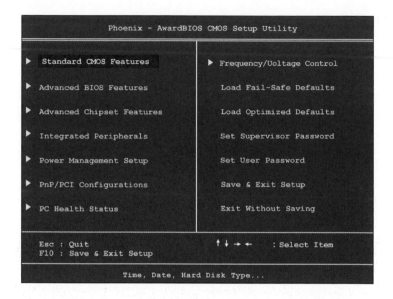

Hot tip

The two main BIOS manufacturers – AWARD and AMI – use slightly different layouts. They are, however, essentially the same. Note that the Illustrations in this chapter are taken from an AWARD BIOS.

This is the main page and from it you can access pages specific to the various parts of the system. Note that your mouse will not work when navigating the BIOS; instead you have to use the following keys to scroll through the pages and change settings.

Key	Action
Up arrow	Moves the cursor up
Down arrow	Moves the cursor down
Left arrow	Moves the cursor left
Right arrow	Moves the cursor right
Page Up	Selects a higher value
Page Down	Selects a lower value
Enter	Makes a selection
Escape	Returns to the previous menu
F1	Opens the BIOS Help screen

Setting the Boot Device

When a PC is started, the BIOS first checks and initializes the system's hardware. It then looks for the operating system in one of the drive units. By default, it will check the floppy drive, hard drive and CD drive in that order. If it can't find the operating system in any of them, it stops the boot procedure with an error message (see page 180).

When you come to partition/format the hard drive prior to loading the operating system, the BIOS must be configured to look at the CD drive first – see top margin note. Do it as described below.

1 On the main BIOS page, scroll to Advanced BIOS Features and press Enter

2 On the next page, scroll down to First Boot Device. Using the Page Up/Page Down keys, cycle through the options and select the required drive

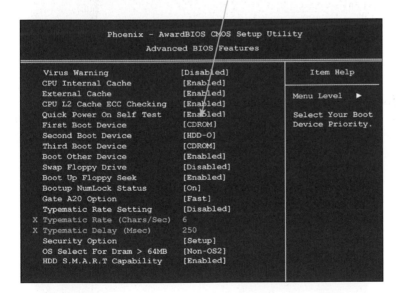

```
         Phoenix - AwardBIOS CMOS Setup Utility
                  Advanced BIOS Features

   Virus Warning                [Disabled]        Item Help
   CPU Internal Cache           [Enabled]
   External Cache               [Enabled]       Menu Level   ▶
   CPU L2 Cache ECC Checking     [Enabled]
   Quick Power On Self Test      [Enabled]      Select Your Boot
   First Boot Device            [CDROM]         Device Priority.
   Second Boot Device           [HDD-O]
   Third Boot Device            [CDROM]
   Boot Other Device            [Enabled]
   Swap Floppy Drive            [Disabled]
   Boot Up Floppy Seek          [Enabled]
   Bootup NumLock Status        [On]
   Gate A20 Option              [Fast]
   Typematic Rate Setting       [Disabled]
 X Typematic Rate (Chars/Sec)    6
 X Typematic Delay (Msec)        250
   Security Option              [Setup]
   OS Select For Dram > 64MB    [Non-OS2]
   HDD S.M.A.R.T Capability     [Enabled]
```

3 Press the Escape key to return to the main page

Note that you must save the change before exiting the BIOS, otherwise it will revert to the original setting. The option for this is on the main BIOS page at the right-hand side (Save & Exit Setup).

Hot tip

With Windows XP and Windows Vista, the partitioning and formatting tools are on the installation disk. Therefore, the system needs to boot from the CD drive in order to access them.

Don't forget

Before you exit the BIOS, save your changes. A quick way is to press the F10 key. This works with both AWARD and AMI BIOSs.

Setting Up the Hard Drive

The first step in setting up the system is to get the hard drive operational by partitioning and then formatting it. With both Windows XP and Windows Vista, these processes are part of the respective operating system's installation procedure.

Before you start though, you must first configure the system to boot from the CD drive as described on page 159.

Windows XP

If you're going to install XP, do the following:

1 Reboot the PC with the XP disk in the CD drive. When you see a message that says "Press any key to boot from CD....", do so. You'll see the following screen

2 Press Enter to begin the installation and then work through the screens that follow until you see the installation options screen, as shown below

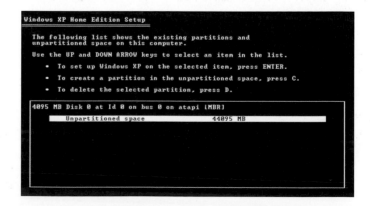

...cont'd

In the lower half of the screen, highlighted in white, you will see details of the drive, or drives, showing where XP can be installed. Because the hard drive is new and hasn't been partitioned yet, all you will see is the unpartitioned space.

3 Press Enter to automatically create a single partition equal to the size of the drive. You will then be taken to the format screen as shown below. Select the file system you want to use – FAT or NTFS – and press Enter. XP will then format the newly created partition

```
Windows XP Home Edition Setup

A new partition for Windows XP has been created on

4095 MB Disk 0 at Id 0 on bus 0 on atapi [MBR].

This partition must now be formatted.

From the list below, select a file system for the new partition.
Use the UP and DOWN ARROW keys to select the file system you want,
and then press ENTER.

If you want to select a different partition for Windows XP,
press ESC.

    Format the partition using the NTFS file system (Quick)
    Format the partition using the FAT file system (Quick)
    Format the partition using the NTFS file system
    Format the partition using the FAT file system
```

When the formatting procedure has completed, XP's installation routine will automatically begin copying files to the hard drive. From this point on, simply follow the prompts as they appear until the installation is complete. On a reasonably well specified machine, the whole process should take about 30 minutes.

Note that if you want to create two or more partitions, then press C in Step 2 on page 160. This will open the partitioning screen where you can create your partitions manually. You can create as many as you like and in any size, as long as the total space allocated is equal to or less than the drive's maximum unpartitioned space.

Windows Vista

When you see the "Press key to boot from CD...." message, do so.

1 At the first screen, select your preferences – installation language, time and currency format and keyboard layout

Hot tip

XP allows you to format the drive in one of two file systems – NTFS or FAT. Unless you are planning to make use of XP's multi-boot facility that allows two or more operating systems to be installed on the PC, choose the NTFS option. Without going into the reasons, this will be the best choice.

You also have the option of doing a "Quick" format. Only use this if the drive is brand new, as the option does not check the disk for errors such as bad sectors.

161

...cont'd

2 Enter the product key and OK the license agreement

3 At the "Which type of installation do you want" screen, select Custom (advanced)

4 At the next screen, "Where do you want to install Windows", click Drive Options (advanced)

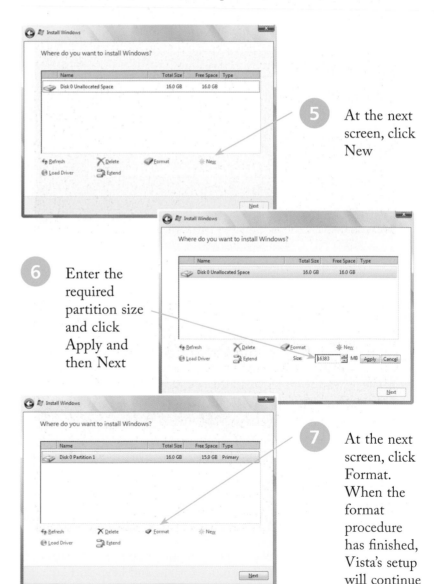

5 At the next screen, click New

6 Enter the required partition size and click Apply and then Next

7 At the next screen, click Format. When the format procedure has finished, Vista's setup will continue

Hot tip

Unlike XP, when the formatting procedure is finished, the Vista installation will complete without any further input from the user. So step 7 will be the last action you need make.

Enabling USB

Next, enable USB. For some reason, many BIOSs come with it disabled.

1 On the main BIOS page, select Integrated Peripherals and press Enter

```
            Phoenix - AwardBIOS CMOS Setup Utility

 ▶ Standard CMOS Features          ▶ Frequency/Voltage Control

 ▶ Advanced BIOS Features            Load Fail-Safe Defaults

 ▶ Advanced Chipset Features         Load Optimized Defaults

 ▶ Integrated Peripherals            Set Supervisor Password

 ▶ Power Management Setup            Set User Password

 ▶ PnP/PCI Configurations            Save & Exit Setup

 ▶ PC Health Status                  Exit Without Saving

 Esc : Quit                  ↑↓ → ←     : Select Item
 F10 : Save & Exit Setup

              Onboard IO, IRQ, DMA Assignment ...
```

2 Scroll to Onchip PCI Device and press Enter

```
            Phoenix - AwardBIOS CMOS Setup Utility
                  Integrated Peripherals

                                              Item Help

 ▶ Via Onchip IDE Device    [Press Enter]
 ▶ Via Onchip PCI Device    [Press Enter]   Menu Level   ▶
 ▶ Super IO Device          [Press Enter]
   Init Display First       [PCI Slot]
```

...cont'd

3 Scroll to Onchip USB Controller and select Enabled

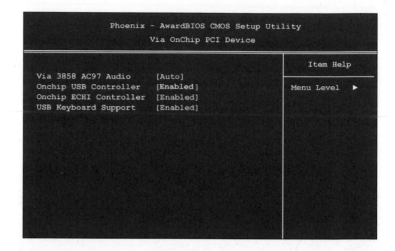

Disabling Integrated Sound

All motherboards come with the integrated sound system enabled by default in the BIOS. If you intend to use a sound card, you must disable it.

1 With the Onchip PCI Device menu still open, scroll to the audio option and select Disabled

Don't forget

If you are planning to use a sound card in your computer, it will be necessary to disable the motherboard's integrated sound system.

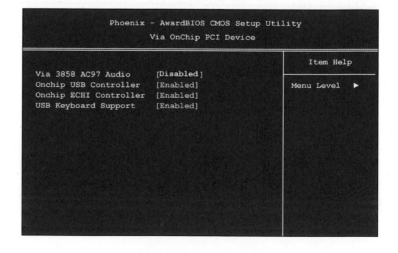

Setting Up a Video Card

When a video card is installed, the interface it uses usually has to be selected in the BIOS; this applies to both AGP and PCI-Express cards.

Do it as described below:

1 On the main BIOS page, select Advanced BIOS Features and press Enter

2 On the next page, scroll to "Init Display First". Using the Page Up/Page Down keys, select the relevant option (AGP or PCI-Express) and then press Enter.

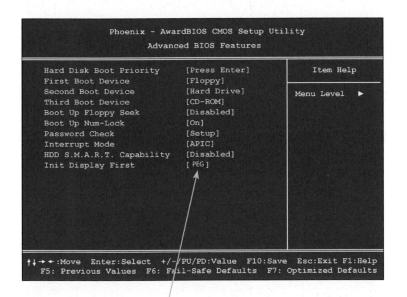

```
                Phoenix - AwardBIOS CMOS Setup Utility
                      Advanced BIOS Features

   Hard Disk Boot Priority    [Press Enter]        Item Help
   First Boot Device          [Floppy]
   Second Boot Device         [Hard Drive]      Menu Level   ►
   Third Boot Device          [CD-ROM]
   Boot Up Floppy Seek        [Disabled]
   Boot Up Num-Lock           [On]
   Password Check             [Setup]
   Interrupt Mode             [APIC]
   HDD S.M.A.R.T. Capability  [Disabled]
   Init Display First         [ PEG ]




   ↑↓→←:Move  Enter:Select  +/-/PU/PD:Value  F10:Save  Esc:Exit F1:Help
     F5: Previous Values  F6: Fail-Safe Defaults  F7: Optimized Defaults
```

Note that PCI-Express may be indicated by the term PEG (PCI-Express Graphics), as shown above.

Be aware that in some BIOSs, there is no option to enable the video card's interface. With these, the correct interface is enabled automatically by the act of physically installing the card in the PC.

The final step is installing the drivers – see margin note and page 166 for more details.

Installing System Drivers

When you run the operating system for the first time, this is the stage at which setting up is completed by the installation of essential system drivers.

Video and Sound Card Drivers
The first are video and sound card drivers. Windows will detect these devices automatically and open the Add Hardware wizard. All you have to do is place the relevant installation disk in the CD drive and Windows will find and install the driver. To complete the installation, you will be asked to reboot the PC.

Motherboard Drivers
When the PC restarts, run the motherboard installation disk; a setup utility similar to the one shown below will open.

Hot tip

Note that you will have video even if the video card driver is not installed. However, the video will be of poor quality as it will be driven by a generic driver provided by Windows.

It's only when you install the driver from the card's installation disk that you will get high-quality video.

Typically, this will provide the following options:

- Chipset drivers for integrated video and sound systems, USB and AGP/PCI-Express interfaces

- Local Area Network (LAN) controller driver

- SATA and RAID drivers

Click the various options to select and install the drivers required.

15 Peripherals

In this chapter, we take a look at the more common types of peripheral, such as scanners and printers and explain what you need to look for to ensure you get a good quality device that will be suitable for your requirements. We also look at dial-up and broadband modems, devices essential for an Internet connection.

Printers

Printers suitable for PC users come in two basic types: ink-jets and lasers. Both have pros and cons that make them suitable for some purposes and less so for others.

Standard Ink-Jet Printers
These printers can be considered to be all-rounders as they produce good results with both text and images. This, together with their low price, makes them the ideal printer for home users.

They do have some drawbacks, however:

- Print quality for both text and images, while perfectly adequate for most purposes, is not the best

- Print speeds are slow; this makes them unsuitable for large-scale print jobs

- The ink cartridges are extremely expensive, which makes these printers suitable for occasional use only

When buying an ink-jet, consider the following:

Print Resolution (dpi)
Letter quality requires a resolution of 600 dpi, while images need one of 1200. All current ink-jets are capable of both but be aware that high-quality photograph printing will require a resolution much higher than 1200 dpi.

Paper Handling
Mainstream ink-jets will print letter size or smaller. If you need to print larger documents, you will need to buy a business class model, which will be considerably more expensive. If you envisage having long print jobs, check out the capacity of the paper input tray. Low-end models will hold no more than 50 sheets or so; high-end models will hold about 150.

Print Speed
This is quoted as pages per minute (PPM), for both color and black and white. Use this specification for comparison purposes only though, as it rarely reflects real world performance.

Build Quality
Printers at the low-end of the market tend to be flimsy affairs. If you buy one of these, expect to be replacing it before too long.

Photo Printers

With the increasing use of PCs for storing and editing images, photo printers have become extremely popular. They also use ink-jet technology but take it to a different level in terms of print quality.

Beware

Note that most photo printers are not so good at printing text, as they are designed for smooth color blending rather than sharp lines. That said, if your requirements aren't too high in this respect, most of them are quite adequate.

They achieve this by using much higher print resolutions and by using a wider range of colored inks than standard ink-jets do. As a result, print quality approaches that of professional print labs.

Photo printers are also quicker than standard ink-jets, which can take an eternity to print a photo at a high setting. Another feature they offer is the ability to read directly from flash memory cards, such as those used by digital cameras. Many also offer an LCD to view your photos, not to mention editing facilities such as crop, rotate, brightness and contrast adjustment, etc.

Things to look out for when buying a photo printer include:

Ink Cartridges

Photo printers, typically, use between four and six different inks, and generally, the ones that use six will produce higher quality prints than those which use less.

You should also be aware that some use a single cartridge that contains all the inks, so if one color runs out, the cartridge has to be replaced even though the other colors haven't. Therefore, running costs can be cut substantially by choosing a model in which each color is held in a separate cartridge.

Memory Card Reader

If you want to take advantage of the direct printing facility offered by these printers, make sure it can read the type of memory card that you use. In particular, look for PictBridge support.

Print Size

Some photo printers have a maximum print size of 4 x 6 inches. If you want larger sizes, be sure to check the specifications.

Hot tip

PictBridge is a standardized technology that lets you transfer images from the memory card in a digital camera directly to a printer. Print size, layout, date, and other settings can be set within the camera. However, both the printer and the camera must support PictBridge.

...cont'd

Laser Printers

Laser technology is completely different from ink-jet and produces much better results in terms of print speed and quality. Laser printers also offer much more in the way of features, such

as high-capacity paper trays and duplexing (a facility that allows printing on both sides of the paper).

They also have much lower running costs than ink-jets.

The main drawback is the higher initial cost, although it must be said that low-end monochrome (black and white) lasers are now similarly priced to ink-jets.

Another drawback is the fact that low-end models are not as good at printing high-quality photographs as photo ink-jets are (you will need at least a mid-range laser for this).

However, if you do serious amounts of printing, or require very high text quality then a laser printer has to be the choice.

If you decide to buy one of these devices, apart from the considerations already mentioned on page 168, you should look at the following:

Toner and Drum

These are the two main consumables in a laser printer. With some lasers, the toner (laser equivalent of ink) and drum are combined in a replaceable cartridge, while with others they are separate parts. The problem with the cartridge type is that the toner will run out long before the drum needs to be replaced. While some cartridges can be refilled with toner, others can't, so to keep running costs down avoid the latter.

Memory

Laser printers come with built-in memory but low-end models are often supplied with a minimal amount of it – usually just enough to allow low-resolution printing. So check that you can upgrade the memory should it be necessary to do so.

Printer Summary

For general purpose use where high-quality is not important, a standard ink-jet will be fine.

For high-quality photo printing, go for a photo printer.

For high-quality text, or large-scale print jobs, a laser printer will be the best choice.

For high-quality text and photos, you will need both a laser and a photo printer, or a mid-range laser. Our recommendation here would be the latter.

Hot tip

A useful advantage color lasers have over ink-jets is that they do not need expensive glossy paper to print high-quality photos. Prints look just as good on matt paper.

Installing a Printer

Printers are simple devices to install – as long as you follow the manufacturer's instructions. Typically, they will be as follows:

1 Install the printer's driver from the installation disk

2 Connect the printer's USB cable to the computer

Don't forget

Make sure that you read the printer's installation instructions. While the procedure described on the left is typical for most current printers, it's not set in stone.

3 Switch the printer on

Windows will then recognize and configure the device, after which it will be ready for use. If you don't follow the above sequence, you may well experience problems.

Multi-Function Devices

Multi-function units consist of a printer and a scanner, which also combine to act as a copier and sometimes a fax machine, all incorporated within the same housing.

The advantages they offer are convenience (one connection to the PC, one wall socket required), less desktop space than would be required by stand-alone devices and a cost saving compared to buying the devices separately. These make them a very attractive option to many users.

The big disadvantage (potentially) is that if something goes wrong with the machine, the user may well lose all of its functions. In a business environment this could well be seriously inconvenient.

As regards buying one, you should look at the specifications of each incorporated device just as you would when buying stand-alone devices.

Beware

A potential problem with multi-function devices is that if they go wrong, the user may lose all the functions that they provide.

Dial-Up Modems

Probably the main factor regarding the quality of a dial-up connection is not the modem itself but rather the telephone line. A noisy and/or low-gain line can be, and often is, the cause of slow or frequently dropped connections.

For this reason, we advise you not to worry about the specifications of these devices – if the line is good, any of the modems currently on the market will do the job. Instead, focus on the features on offer. These include:

V Standard

The modem must use the latest V standard – V.92. While in terms of speed (operating at 56 KB/s), it is no faster than its predecessor, V.90, it does offer some extra features, such as quicker establishment of a connection and being able to make and receive telephone calls without breaking the connection.

Internet Telephone Capability

If the modem is Internet phone ready, you will be able to make reduced cost, or even free, international calls. Note that this requires a software program from a service provider such as Skype (www.skype.com).

A useful feature in this regard is speakerphone capability, which provides an interface for a microphone and speaker or headset.

Integrated Processor

A built-in micro-processor handles the processing for your connection, so the PC's CPU doesn't have to do the work. This optimizes connections to graphic intensive sites such as online gaming and streaming audio/video. Cheap modems don't have a processor.

Software

A good software package will include applications for streaming audio and video over the Internet, online games, faxing and answering the telephone, etc.

External Models

Another consideration is to buy an external, rather than internal, model. This will release a PCI socket for another device. A further advantage is that external modems have a number of LEDs, which can be useful when troubleshooting connection problems.

Beware

One of the features offered by V.92 modems is "Modem-on-hold". This allows users to make and receive phone calls without losing the Internet connection. However, the feature needs to be supported by the ISP, so check that yours does.

Hot tip

Buy a modem that has a "flashable" memory chip, as opposed to a ROM chip. A flash chip will enable you to update the modem periodically by downloading a firmware upgrade from the manufacturer's website.

Installing a Dial-Up Modem

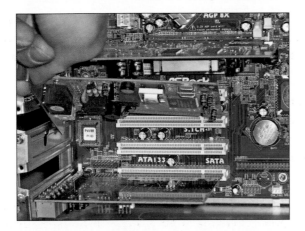

1 Slide the modem into a PCI socket

2 Press it home and screw the face plate to the chassis

3 Connect one end of the data cable to the modem's output socket

4 Connect the other end to the phone jack

Don't forget

To complete the installation, install the modem's driver when back in Windows.

Broadband Modems

Broadband Modems

If broadband is available in your area, you ought to seriously consider signing up for it. It has many advantages and will revolutionize the way you use the Internet.

Broadband comes in several versions, each of which require the use of a specialized modem.

- DSL and ADSL – works on telephone lines with speeds up to 10 MB/s (although few ISPs offer anything higher than 4 or 5 MB/s)

- Cable – works on CATV cable networks and provides similar speeds to DSL and ADSL

- Satellite – for people living in remote locations, a satellite connection is an option. It is available with speeds of up to 2 MB/s. It is expensive though and is also the least reliable as it can be adversely affected by weather conditions

Of the three types, cable is the one recommended as it is the easiest to set up and also the most reliable. However, not everyone has access to a cable network and if this is the case, DSL is the next best option.

The modem will connect to the computer via either USB or Ethernet. For simplicity of installation, USB is the easiest. An Ethernet connection will also require an Ethernet PCI card to be installed in the PC, unless the motherboard has an integrated Ethernet interface – many do these days.

Virtually all ISPs will supply a modem as part of the package (and charge you rental accordingly), so this is not something you need to consider unless of course you buy your own modem, which may allow you to negotiate a lower price with the ISP.

With regard to specifications, as with dial-up modems, this is not something you need to investigate.

A feature available with some modems that's worth having, is a built-in hardware firewall. Firewalls are essential for broadband connections and most people use a software version, which tend not to be as good as a hardware firewall.

Hot tip

If you decide to sign-up for a broadband package, which will usually include a modem, there is nothing to stop you from buying one yourself and negotiating a better deal with the ISP. However, you should check with the ISP first – for technical reasons, some may insist on using their own modem.

Hot tip

If you are fortunate enough to have a choice, cable broadband is the recommended option. It's quick, reliable and easy to set up.

Installing a Broadband Modem

The first step is to extend the signal input from its entry point of the house, to where the modem is located. For this you will need a suitable length of coaxial cable and the appropriate connectors.

If you are tapping into your TV's cable input, you will also need a signal splitter, as shown above. Connect the signal cable to the splitter's input, connect the TV to one output and the modem's cable to the other output. Then run the latter to the modem.

Don't forget

If you are connecting an Ethernet modem to a Ethernet adapter built-in to the motherboard, remember that it will be necessary to install the Ethernet driver from the motherboard's installation disk.

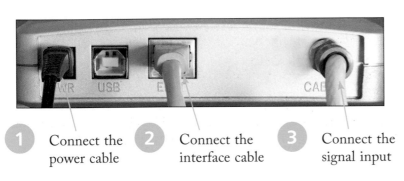

1 Connect the power cable

2 Connect the interface cable

3 Connect the signal input

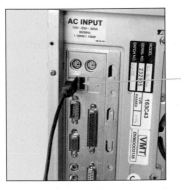

4 Connect the modem (a USB model in this example) to the PC

Don't forget

When running your new modem for the first time, be aware that it may need several minutes to synchronize itself with the network. During this period, you will be unable to access the Internet.

5 Switch the PC on, and when in Windows run the installation disk. Windows will detect the device and load its driver from the disk. Note that it's not essential to load the ISP's software – the driver is all that's needed to establish the connection. However, we suggest that you do as the software may include useful functions, such as a diagnostic program in case of connection problems.

Scanners

Scanners are devices that are by no means essential, but can turn out to be surprisingly useful in many ways. For home-users, the flatbed type (shown right) is the best one to go for.

When deciding which scanner to buy, you need to consider the following specifications:

Resolution

This is a measure of how much detail is reproduced by the scan process and is expressed in dots per inch (dpi). The table below shows the resolution required by the most common applications.

Application	Resolution
Images for commercial printing	300 dpi
Images to be enlarged	300 dpi upwards
Negatives and Slides	1200 dpi minimum
Images for printing on ink-jet printers	200 to 300 dpi
Text documents	300 dpi
Line art (drawings, diagrams, etc)	300 dpi
Images for websites, viewing on monitors	72 dpi

Optical Density

Also known as Dynamic Range, this indicates how wide a range of tones the scanner can recognize and is measured on a scale from 0.0 (perfect white) to 4.0 (perfect black).

Most flatbed scanners have an OD around 2.8 to 3.0, which is fine for photographs. Slides, negatives and transparencies, which have broader tonal ranges, will need a higher OD of about 3.4.

Interface

SCSI (requires a SCSI adapter) is the ideal for speed. Next best is USB (USB 2 ideally). Avoid Parallel Port (if you can find a scanner that still uses it), as this is the slowest.

Accessories

Some scanners include useful accessories such as slide and negative attachments and sheet feeders.

Speakers

A good set of speakers is an essential part of a high-quality sound system. You may have the best sound card in the galaxy but if it is connected to a cheap speaker system, you will get poor sound.

PC speakers are available either as a pair or as a multiple speaker system. The type of setup you go for depends on the intended use.

Music buffs who simply want high-fidelity will be best served by a pair of high-quality stereo speakers – a surround-sound system is not necessary.

Gamers and DVD movie fans who do want surround-sound will need a multiple speaker system, as shown below. When buying one of these, don't forget to check that your sound system

 is capable of fully utilizing it. There's no point in buying a 7.1 speaker system if you have only three line-out jacks, for example.

Whichever type of setup you go for, considering the following

specifications will ensure that your chosen speakers are up to scratch.

Frequency Response
This is the range of frequencies that the speakers can reproduce. The closer it is to the 20 Hz (bass) and 20 KHz (treble) thresholds, the better the output quality.

Sensitivity
This is sometimes referred to as Sound Pressure Level in specification sheets and indicates the efficiency with which the speakers convert power to sound. Look for a figure of at least 90 decibels.

Wattage Rating
While this is not a true indication of quality, it is a fact that speakers with a high wattage rating do generally produce better sound.

177

Hot tip

The wider a speaker's frequency range, the better its quality. Low-frequency response is essential for good bass reproduction, while high-frequency response is essential for good treble reproduction.

Hot tip

Speaker wattage is rated in two ways: peak power and continuous (RMS) power. The manufacturers like to emphasize the former as this is the higher of the two figures. However, buyers should be more concerned with the continuous power rating as this gives a more accurate indication of the speaker's capabilities.

Speaker Installation

This is a simple enough exercise. However, it is remarkable how many people get it wrong, connecting the speakers to either the wrong sound system (integrated instead of the sound card or vice versa) or to the wrong jack.

The input/output ports of a basic sound card are shown below:

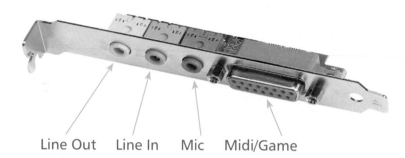

Line Out   Line In   Mic   Midi/Game

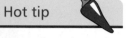

Hot tip

Most sound cards provide color-coded input and output jacks for easy identification.

Green – line out
Orange – line out
Black – line out
Blue – line in
Pink – microphone

The speakers connect to the green line out jack. Use any other jack and you will not get any sound from the PC. With the card shown above you will only be able to use a two-speaker setup.

Advanced sound cards offer more in the way of connectivity as demonstrated by the input/output panel of the card shown below:

Hot tip

S/PDIF stands for Sony/Philips Digital Interface; a standard audio file transfer format. Developed jointly by the Sony and Phillips corporations, S/PDIF allows the transfer of digital audio signals from one device to another without having to be first converted to an analog format, which has a degrading effect on the quality of the signal.

Here, the green, black and two orange jacks all provide a line out connection. The pink jack is for a microphone, the blue jack is for line in, and finally, there are input and output sockets for S/PDIF coaxial cables – see margin note.

In multiple speaker setups, the green line out jack is used for the front speakers, the black jack for the rear speakers and the orange jacks for the center and side speakers.

As it has four line out jacks, the card shown above can support eight speakers.

16 Troubleshooting

If all goes to plan, you won't need to read this chapter. However, you may encounter a problem or two somewhere along the way and our purpose here is to provide a solution if you do.

Hard Drives

Hard Drive Failure

When you boot-up the computer, on the first boot screen you should see the hard drive listed next to "Primary Master" (in the case of an ATA drive) as shown below, or next to "RAID Controller" (in the case of a SATA drive).

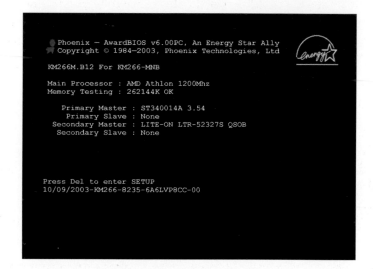

```
   Phoenix — AwardBIOS v6.00PC, An Energy Star Ally
   Copyright © 1984—2003, Phoenix Technologies, Ltd

   KM266M.B12 For KM266-MNB

   Main Processor : AMD Athlon 1200Mhz
   Memory Testing : 262144K OK

      Primary Master : ST340014A 3.54
       Primary Slave : None
    Secondary Master : LITE-ON LTR-52327S QSOB
     Secondary Slave : None



   Press Del to enter SETUP
   10/09/2003-KM266-8235-6A6LVP8CC-00
```

If it isn't there, the PC isn't "seeing" it. Depending on the BIOS in your system, one of two things will happen.

1) Boot-up will stop at this point

2) Boot-up will continue and then stop with a "Disk Boot Failure" error message

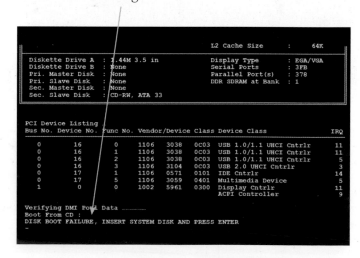

```
                                          L2 Cache Size      :    64K
   Diskette Drive A  : 1.44M 3.5 in        Display Type      : EGA/VGA
   Diskette Drive B  : None                Serial Ports      : 3FB
   Pri. Master Disk  : None                Parallel Port(s)  : 378
   Pri. Slave Disk   : None                DDR SDRAM at Bank : 1
   Sec. Master Disk  : None
   Sec. Slave Disk   : CD-RW, ATA 33


   PCI Device Listing
   Bus No. Device No. Func No. Vendor/Device Class Device Class                IRQ

       0      16       0      1106   3038   0C03  USB 1.0/1.1 UHCI Cntrlr      11
       0      16       1      1106   3038   0C03  USB 1.0/1.1 UHCI Cntrlr      11
       0      16       2      1106   3038   0C03  USB 1.0/1.1 UHCI Cntrlr       5
       0      16       3      1106   3104   0C03  USB 2.0 UHCI Cntrlr           3
       0      17       1      1106   0571   0101  IDE Cntrlr                   14
       0      17       5      1106   3059   0401  Multimedia Device             5
       1       0       0      1002   5961   0300  Display Cntrlr               11
                                                  ACPI Controller               9

   Verifying DMI Pool Data ..............
   Boot From CD :
   DISK BOOT FAILURE, INSERT SYSTEM DISK AND PRESS ENTER
   -
```

There are three possible causes of this:

1) The drive is not powered up
2) The drive is not connected correctly
3) The drive is faulty

The first thing to check is that the drive is getting power from the power supply unit. The easiest way to do this is to connect a different power connector that you know is working; for example, the one powering the CD/DVD drive.

Next, check that the drive is properly connected to the motherboard. Remake the interface connections and check that they are correct – see pages 118-121.

If the drive is getting power and the connections are OK, then the device is faulty. This is very unlikely though and invariably the fault will be a connection issue.

Another problem that can occur is the boot procedure stopping at the "Verifying DMI Pool Data" stage.

```
                                    L2 Cache Size      :      64K

 Diskette Drive A  : 1.44M 3.5 in     Display Type     : EGA/VGA
 Diskette Drive B  : None             Serial Ports     : 3FB
 Pri. Master Disk  : None             Parallel Port(s) : 378
 Pri. Slave Disk   : None             DDR SDRAM at Bank : 1
 Sec. Master Disk  : None
 Sec. Slave Disk   : CD-RW, ATA 33


 PCI Device Listing ...
 Bus No. Device No. Func No. Vendor/Device Class Device Class        IRQ

     0       16        0      1106  3038  0C03  USB 1.0/1.1 UHCI Cntrlr   11
     0       16        1      1106  3038  0C03  USB 1.0/1.1 UHCI Cntrlr   11
     0       16        2      1106  3038  0C03  USB 1.0/1.1 UHCI Cntrlr    5
     0       16        3      1106  3104  0C03  USB 2.0 UHCI Cntrlr        3
     0       17        1      1106  0571  0101  IDE Cntrlr                14
     0       17        5      1106  3059  0401  Multimedia Device          5
     1        0        0      1002  5961  0300  Display Cntrlr            11
                                             ACPI Controller             9

 Verifying DMI Pool Data ..............
 -
```

This can be the result of a transient configuration problem that can usually be resolved by switching off and then back on again.

If the problem persists, it is likely to be a connection issue. Open the system case and remake the interface connection to both the motherboard and hard drive.

Removable Media Drives

Usually, when these devices have a physical problem, the relevant drive icon will be missing in My Computer.

Boot the PC and on the first boot screen you should see the drive listed next to Secondary Master. If it isn't, the drive is either faulty or it has a connection problem. Open the system case and check that the power and interface cables are securely connected. If the interface cable is an older 40-pin cable, try reversing the connection to the drive, as it is possible to connect these the wrong way round. If the BIOS still doesn't recognize the drive, it is faulty.

If the drive is listed on the boot screen but not in My Computer then it has a configuration problem (see margin note). See if the drive is listed in Device Manager under the DVD/CD-ROM category and whether any problems are reported there. If so, try the suggested remedy. Failing that, do the following:

 In the Device Manager, right-click the device and click Uninstall

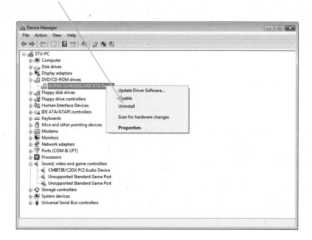

 Switch the PC off and physically disconnect the drive by removing both the power and interface cables. Then reconnect them and reboot. Windows will see the device as a new addition to the system and automatically assign it a new channel, which should resolve the issue

If the drive isn't listed in Device Manager, follow the procedure described in Step 2 above.

Hot tip

Drive configuration issues relate to the communication channels assigned by Windows that enable the drive to communicate with the CPU. These problems can usually be resolved with the Device Manager (Start, Control Panel, System, Device Manager).

Don't forget

If you have installed two CD/DVD drives in the system and one or both don't work, check that you have correctly positioned the master/slave configuration jumpers at the rear of the units.

Video

Blank Display

If the boot procedure gets as far as the point where Windows begins to load, and then the screen goes blank, the cause is likely to be an AGP video card incorrectly configured in the BIOS.

The setting you need to check is the AGP Aperture Size. Enter the BIOS setup program then go to Advanced Chipset Features, AGP & P2P Bridge Control. Scroll to AGP Aperture Size and select a low setting – [64M] or [32M].

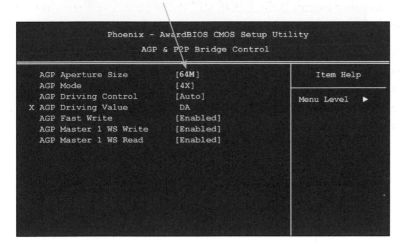

```
              Phoenix - AwardBIOS CMOS Setup Utility
                    AGP & P2P Bridge Control

    AGP Aperture Size          [64M]            Item Help
    AGP Mode                   [4X]
    AGP Driving Control        [Auto]        Menu Level   ▶
  X AGP Driving Value          DA
    AGP Fast Write             [Enabled]
    AGP Master 1 WS Write      [Enabled]
    AGP Master 1 WS Read       [Enabled]
```

Save the change, reboot and the video should now be working.

Video is Slow

By this we mean that the video system is drawing the picture on the display noticeably slowly. This is a sure sign that the video driver hasn't been installed, is incorrect or is corrupt. You will also find that the screen resolution and color depth cannot be changed. The solution is to install or re-install, the correct driver.

Scrambled Display

Another problem that can occur when a video card is installed, is being greeted by a scrambled (an unintelligible mass of colored lines) display when the PC is booted. This is usually caused by the display's refresh rate being too high. Resolve it as follows:

 Reboot the PC and immediately start tapping the F8 key. After a few moments, the Advanced Boot Options menu will open

...cont'd

When a PC is run in Safe Mode, many hardware drivers are not loaded, which eliminates most of the problems likely to stop Windows running.

To produce video, Windows loads a basic "no frills" video driver that works with all setups. Then you can use the troubleshooting tools provided by Windows to resolve the issue, whatever it may be.

Hot tip

If the display is flickering noticeably, select a higher refresh rate as described opposite.

2 Scroll to Safe Mode and press Enter

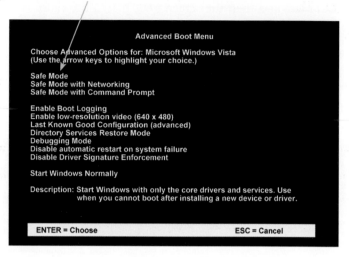

The PC will continue to boot. When Windows starts, you will notice that it runs slowly and that many of its functions are disabled. This is because most of the system's drivers (including the video driver) are not loaded when in Safe Mode.

3 Go to Start, Control Panel, Personalization. Click Display Settings and Advanced Settings. Then click the Monitor tab

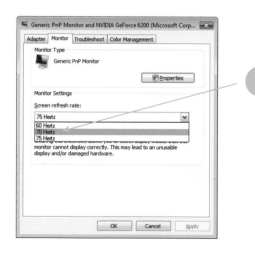

 4 Using the drop-down box, select a lower refresh rate

Reboot and all should now be well.

Sound

If you are not getting any sound, the first thing to check is that the speakers are connected to the correct output jacks as described on page 178.

If your system has both integrated sound and a sound card, make sure that the speakers are connected to the correct system.

Check that the speakers are powered up and that volume controls, both on the speakers and in Windows, are turned up.

If you are using a sound card, check that the integrated sound system has been disabled in the BIOS as described on page 164.

In the unlikely event that you still have no sound after the above checks, then you have a driver issue. Do the following:

1 Go to Start, Control Panel and Sound

2 On both the Playback and Recording tabs, you will see a message saying "No audio devices are installed"

3 Install or reinstall the sound driver. In the case of integrated sound, install it from the motherboard's installation disk and in the case of a sound card, install it from the card's installation disk

Hot tip

If you are using an integrated sound system, the speakers will need a separate power supply.

Make sure they are plugged in and that the speaker's volume control is turned up.

Hot tip

If you are not getting any sound from your CD/DVD drive, check that you have connected the drive's audio cable to the PC's sound system.

Dial-Up Modems

Problems with broadband modems are rare and are almost always due to simple connection issues. Dial-up modems, however, can be a real pain to get operational, so we'll concentrate on these.

If the modem won't dial out, check the following:

First, is the driver installed correctly. Open the Device Manager (Start, Control Panel, System, Device Manager) and check that the modem is listed under the Modem category. If it isn't or there is no Modem category, install or reinstall the driver.

Second, do a modem diagnostic check. Right-click the modem in the Device Manager and select Properties. In the dialog box that opens, click the Diagnostics tab and then click Query Modem.

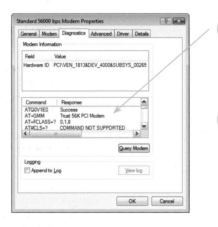

1 A list of AT commands indicates that the device is OK and that you have a software problem

2 In the Control Panel, open the Network and Sharing Center. Click Manage Network Connections, right-click the modem connection and click Delete

3 Now reinstall the connection using the disk supplied by your ISP

If the modem dials out now, then its communication configuration was corrupt. If it still doesn't work and its connections are OK, then it is almost certainly faulty.

If, however, the AT commands don't appear in the diagnostic test, the problem is likely to be a hardware issue. Check all physical connections to and from the modem. If you get an error message, such as "the modem failed to respond", Windows may have set up the modem on the wrong COM port. Uninstalling and reinstalling the modem driver should resolve the issue.

Index

T

U

V

W

Z